Reading Skills Competency Tests

FOURTH LEVEL

Walter B. Barbe, Ph.D.

A nationally-known authority in the areas of reading and learning disabilities, Walter B. Barbe, Ph.D., is editor-in-chief of the widely acclaimed magazine, *Highlights for Children,* and adjunct professor at The Ohio State University. Dr. Barbe is the author of over 150 professional articles and a number of books, including *Personalized Reading Instruction* (West Nyack, NY: Parker Publishing Co., Inc., 1975), coauthored with Jerry L. Abbott. He is also the senior author and editor of two series: *Creative Growth with Handwriting* (Columbus, Ohio: Zaner-Bloser, Inc., 1975) and the *Barbe Reading Skills Check Lists and Activities* (West Nyack, NY: The Center for Applied Research in Education, Inc., 1976). Dr. Barbe is a fellow of the American Psychological Association and is listed in *Who's Who in America* and *American Men of Science.*

Henriette L. Allen, Ph.D.

Henriette L. Allen, Ph.D., a former classroom teacher in the Coventry, Rhode Island, schools, Aramco Schools of Dhahran, Saudi Arabia, and The American Community School of Benghazi, Libya, is presently an administrative assistant to the superintendent with the Jackson, Mississippi, Public Schools. She has taught reading skills at elementary and secondary levels and supervised the development of a Continuous Progress Reading Program for the Jackson Public Schools. Dr. Allen has lectured widely in the fields of reading, classroom management, and leadership in educational administration. She is listed in the *World Who's Who of Women* and *Who's Who—School District Officials.*

COMPETENCY TESTS FOR BASIC READING SKILLS

The Center for Applied Research in Education, Inc.
West Nyack, New York 10994

Printed in the United States of America

About the *Competency Tests for Basic Reading Skills*

The Reading Skills Competency Tests are a practical tool designed to provide classroom teachers, reading specialists, Title I teachers and others an inventory of those reading skills mastered and those which need to be taught. The tests can be used at all levels with any reading program, as they test mastery of specific reading skills at particular levels.

For easiest use, the test materials are organized into eight distinct units tailored to evaluate children's reading skills at each of the following expectancy and difficulty levels:

Reading Skills Competency Tests: READINESS LEVEL
Reading Skills Competency Tests: FIRST LEVEL
Reading Skills Competency Tests: SECOND LEVEL
Reading Skills Competency Tests: THIRD LEVEL
Reading Skills Competency Tests: FOURTH LEVEL
Reading Skills Competency Tests: FIFTH LEVEL
Reading Skills Competency Tests: SIXTH LEVEL
Reading Skills Competency Tests: ADVANCED LEVEL

The tests give reading teachers a quick, informal means to measure the mastery of reading objectives. They can be used at any time to assess the student's competence in specific reading skills, to pinpoint specific skill weaknesses and problems, and to plan appropriate corrective or remedial instruction in an individualized reading program.

The sequence of the tests corresponds to the sequence of the well-known "Barbe Reading Skills Check Lists," which provide a complete developmental skill sequence from Readiness through Advanced Levels. Each level-unit presents ready-to-use informal tests for evaluating all skills that are listed on the Skills Check List at that level. Tests can be administered individually or to a group by a teacher or a paraprofessional.

Each unit of test materials contains:

1. Directions for using the Reading Skills Competency Tests at that grade level to identify individual reading needs and prescribe appropriate instruction.
2. Copies of the Skills Check List and a Group Summary Profile at that grade level for use in individual and group recordkeeping.

3. Reading Skills Competency Tests for assessing all skills at that particular grade level, including teacher test sheets with directions and answer keys for administering and evaluating each test plus reproducible student test sheets.

Note: The student test sheets are also available from the publisher on duplicating masters.

4. A duplicating master of the Skills Check List at the particular grade level for setting up individual skills records for all children in a class.
5. A copy of the "Barbe Reading Skills Sequential Skill Plan" chart.

For easy use of the materials, complete directions are provided in each unit for using the Competency Tests at that level and for recording the information on the student skills Check List and the Group Summary Profile.

The test items in each level unit correspond to the skills indicated on the Check List. The Check List can be marked to indicate which skills the child has mastered or the skills in which further instruction is needed. The Group Summary Profile can be used to obtain an overall picture of class progress and to identify the skills which need to be taught. It is also useful in identifying small groups with similar needs, students who require personalized help on a prerequisite skill, and students who need continued help on a current skill.

You will find that these tests provide for:

- quick, informal assessment of students' competence in reading skills
- diagnosis and prescription of specific reading skill weaknesses and needs
- devising of appropriate teaching strategies for individuals and small or large groups
- continuous evaluation of each child's progress in the basic reading skills
- flexibility in planning the reading instructional program
- immediate feedback to the student and the teacher

The Competency Tests for Basic Reading Skills can be used by all reading teachers in either a self-contained classroom or a team setting. They are as flexible as the teacher chooses to make them. Hopefully, they will provide an efficient, systematic means to identify the specific reading skills that students need to learn and thus meet to a greater degree, their individual reading needs.

Henriette L. Allen

Walter B. Barbe

Contents

How to Use the Competency Tests and Check List

A major task for teachers is verifying mastery of basic skills and keeping records. Recordkeeping and competency tests are of greater concern today than ever before. But knowing of their necessity does not make the task any easier. Competency tests and the accompanying records may be compared to a road map. One must drive through Town B to reach Town W. Competency tests are designed to assist you in verifying mastery of basic reading skills, and to indicate where to begin on the journey of reading mastery. The Reading Skills Check Lists provide check points to verify (1) where the student is on the sequence of skills, (2) when the skills were mastered, and (3) at what rate he or she is progressing.

In order for skills to develop sequentially, it is vital that we have an idea of where a student is within the sequence of reading skills. The Reading Skills Competency Tests and Check List in this unit are designed to help you teach directly to identified student needs, on a day-to-day, week-to-week, and month-to-month basis.

The Reading Skills Competency Tests are easy-to-administer tests for each reading skill on the "Barbe Reading Skills Check Lists." Directions for administering each test are given on a teacher page. This page also provides the answer key and the number of correct responses needed for mastery. Facing the teacher page is the student test page, which can be used as a master for copying when reproduction for classroom use is via copy machine. The student tests are also available on spirit duplicating masters.

The Check Lists are not intended as a rigid program for reading instruction. Rather they are meant to provide a general pattern around which a program may be built. The Fourth Level Skills Check List is divided into four major headings: Vocabulary, Word Attack Skills, Comprehension, and Oral and Silent Reading. Each area is of great importance to the student's development. In presenting the skills on the Check List, it is recommended that you deal alternately with some activities from each of the four major headings.

You will find a copy of the Fourth Level Skills Check List on page 14, and a duplicating master of the Check List at the end of this aid, which you can copy and use for individual recordkeeping.

Begin at the Beginning

Before planning an instructional program for any pupil, it is necessary to determine at what level the student is reading. This may be determined through the use of an informal reading inventory. It is then necessary to identify which basic reading skills the pupil has mastered and which skills need remediation or initial teaching.

The Competency Tests for Basic Reading Skills offer a quick, practical means to determine which skills the student has mastered and on which the student needs additional work. It is suggested that the tests be administered at the beginning of a school year. The tests may also be used at any time throughout the year to determine a student's entry point in a Reading Skills Class, or to reevaluate the progress of individual students. The tests may be given to a large group, a small group, or an individual, whichever is appropriate for those being tested and for the test being administered. Some tests, such as Oral Reading, must be administered individually. The entry point into the reading program should be at that point when a student begins to encounter difficulty with a particular reading skill.

The tests may be used as a pre test to indicate where instruction is needed, and the same tests may also be used as a post test to indicate mastery or non-mastery. Once a pupil's areas of difficulty are identified, you may then plan instructional activities accordingly. After the student has worked through a unit of instruction, you may use the same test to verify mastery of the skill. When mastery occurs, the student is advanced to another skill. When the student is unsuccessful on the specific test item, additional instruction is needed. If a reasonable amount of instruction does not result in mastery, it may be that changing instructional approaches is needed or that more work is needed on earlier skills.

Once you have decided the level of mastery tests needed, the assessing part of the reading program is ready to begin. Specific directions are given for each test. At the Fourth Level, you may assign the test to be taken and permit the students to work independently or you may give the directions to the student. The directions are given at the top of every student test page and on the teacher page. In some instances, as in oral reading, you may have to test each student individually.

Recording on the Check List

Recordkeeping is an important part in any instructional design. Simplicity and ease is vital. One effective method for marking the Skills Check List is as follows:

B. Phonic Analysis			
1. Knows phonic skills			
a. Single consonants and blends	10/28	M	11/3
b. Short and long vowels	M		
c. Vowel teams	11/4	M	11/12
2. Knows vowel rules			
a. Try short sound, then long sound	M		
b. Short when single vowels and followed by consonant			

Put an M in the first column if the pupil takes a test and demonstrates mastery of that basic reading skill. If the pupil has not mastered the skill, record the date. The date in column one indicates when instruction in the skill began. When the pupil is tested a second time, put an M in the second column if mastery is achieved, and record the date of mastery in the third column. Thus, anyone looking at the Check List can tell if the student mastered the skill before instruction or when instruction began, and when the skill was actually mastered. The Check List provides a written record of: (1) where the student is on the sequence of reading skills, (2) when the student mastered the skills, and (3) at what rate the student is progressing.

Conferencing with the Pupil

The student and teacher may discuss performance on the Competency Tests and Check List and jointly plan subsequent instruction. The Check List provides a guide for this discussion.

Conferencing with Parents

The Reading Skills Check List also serves as a guide for parent conferences. Using the Check List you can talk with parents about specific skills mastered, as well as those which have been taught but not yet fully mastered. Use of the Check List reassures parents of your concern for skill instruction, your knowledge of ways to aid their child in becoming a better reader, and of your professional plan which considers each child individually.

Conferencing with Professional Staff

Conferences with other staff such as school psychologists, counselors, and principals concerning an individual child's reading progress should focus on the instructional plan. When Check Lists are used, other professional staff members are provided with a written record of the teacher's progress and the child's progress in this program. The Check List provides information on the skills mastered, and when the skills were mastered.

Providing Check Lists to the Next Grade Level Teacher

One of the great problems in teaching reading skills at the beginning of the year is to know where to begin. If the Reading Skills Check Lists are passed along from class to class, the new teacher will know the skill level of every student in the room.

Making a Group Summary Profile from Individual Check Lists

While the Reading Skills Check List is intended primarily for individual use, there are various reasons for bringing together a record of the instructional needs to the entire class. In planning classroom strategies, you will find the use of the Group Profile on pages 16 through 18 helpful.

After you have recorded the skill level for each student on the Reading Skills Check List, you may then enter this information on the Group Profile. The Group Summary Profile is designed to help you identify groups of students who need a particular skill. It is a visual representation of the instructional needs of the entire class. It also presents the specific strengths and achievement levels of individual students.

The Group Profile may be used in conferences with supervisors and administrators to discuss the status of a particular class, the point of initial instruction, and the progress made to date. A different colored pen or pencil may be used to indicate the different grading or marking periods of the school year. This further indicates the progress the pupils have made within these periods of time.

The Group Profile can indicate the instructional materials and supplies which are needed. Since specific reading skills needs will be clearly identified, materials may be purchased which meet these needs.

Ensuring the Sequential Presentation of Skills

One of the goals of reading instruction is to develop a love of reading. But if students are to develop a love of reading, they must be able to read with efficiency. And in order to be efficient readers they must have at their ready command all of the necessary skills, including the ability to unlock new words and to read rapidly.

If the skills are to be mastered, they must be presented sequentially. When skills are presented out of sequence, critical skills are in danger of being bypassed or given minimal attention.

In many instances, the sequence of skills is firmly established; in other instances the sequence is less rigid. In these Check Lists, the skills have been placed in the order the authors feel is logical. Teachers should be free to change this sequence when there is reason to do so, being careful not to eliminate the presentation of the skill.

It is important that some skill instruction be conducted in groups. This prevents individual students from becoming isolated, a danger which sometimes occurs when too much individualization is undertaken.

Using the Sequential Skill Plan Chart

The importance of viewing the total sequential skills program cannot be minimized. The chart is intended primarily for use by the classroom teacher. If a personalized approach is used in teaching reading skills, it is still essential that the teacher view the skills as a continuous progression rather than as skills for a specific grade level. This chart allows the teacher to view not only those skills that are taught principally at the present grade placement, but also those skills which will be taught as the student progresses.

As an inservice tool, the chart provides teachers with the opportunity to see their own positions in the skills progression. It should be understood, of course, that there are any number of reasons why decisions may be made to teach the skills at levels different from those indicated on the chart. But it is important that reading skills be taught, and that basically they be taught in a sequential manner, in a planned reading program. Incidental teaching of reading skills often results in vital skills being neglected, or being bypassed until the student encounters difficulties. At that point, having to go back to earlier skills is more difficult and less effective.

The chart also provides administrators, supervisors, and teachers with direction for a total skills program.

Reading Skills Check List—Fourth Level

On the following pages you will find a copy of the "Barbe Reading Skills Check List–Fourth Level." The Check List presents a sequential outline of the skills to be mastered at this level in four major areas: Vocabulary, Word Attack Skills, Comprehension, and Oral and Silent Reading.

For use in individual recordkeeping, the Fourth Level Skills Check List is also printed on a spirit duplicating master at the end of this unit.

Accompanying the unit is a copy of the "Barbe Reading Skills Check List Sequential Skill Plan." This chart provides a visual representation of the total reading skills progression through all levels, including:

Readiness Level
First Level
Second Level
Third Level
Fourth Level
Fifth Level
Sixth Level
Advanced Level

BARBE READING SKILLS CHECK LIST
FOURTH LEVEL

(Last Name) (First Name) (Name of School)

(Age) (Grade Placement) (Name of Teacher)

I. Vocabulary:
A. Word Recognition
1. Knows new words in content fields
2. Recognizes similarities of known words
   a. compound words
   b. root words
   c. suffixes, prefixes
   d. plurals
   e. hyphenated words
   f. contractions
3. Recognizes unusual characteristics of words

B. Word Meaning
1. Develops ability in getting meaning from context
2. Uses new words in sentences to show meaning
3. Knows punctuation
   a. italics
   b. quotation marks
   c. parenthesis
   d. exclamation marks
4. Use of map skills

C. Review Dolch Words

II. Word Attack Skills:
A. Structural analysis
1. Knows and applies rules for syllables
   a. Each syllable must contain a vowel and a single vowel can be a syllable
   b. Suffixes and prefixes are syllables with meanings of their own
   c. The root word is not divided
   d. If the first vowel is followed by two consonants, the first syllable usually ends with the first consonant (example: pen cil)
   e. If the first vowel is followed by a single consonant, the consonant usually begins the second syllable (example: a maze, am ple)
   f. If a word ends in le preceded by a consonant, that consonant begins the last syllable
   g. The letter x always goes with the preceding vowel to form a syllable (example: ex it)
   h. The letters ck go with the preceding vowel and end the syllable (example: chick en)
2. Knows accent clues
   a. The first syllable is usually accented, unless it is a prefix
   b. Beginning syllables de, re, be, in and a are usually unaccented
   c. Endings that form syllables are usually unaccented (run ning)
   d. ck following a single vowel is accented (example: jack et)
3. Knows suffixes and prefixes:
   a. Suffixes:

ness	(being)	sickness
ment	(result of)	movement
ward	(in direction of)	backward
ous	(full of)	joyous
ious	(abounding in)	gracious
et	(little)	leaflet
able	(capable of being)	capable
ic	(like, made of)	magic
ish	(like)	foolish
ant	(being)	vacant
ent	(one who)	president
age	(collection of)	baggage
ance	(state of being)	disturbance
ence	(state or quality)	violence
wise	(ways)	crosswise
ling	(little)	duckling
ty	(state)	unity
ure	(denoting action)	pleasure
ion	(condition or quality)	action

   b. Prefixes:

dis	(not, apart)	dismiss
in	(not)	invade
mis	(wrong)	mistake
anti	(against)	anticlimax
non	(not)	nonsense
com	(with)	combine
con	(with)	connect
pre	(before)	prepare
super	(over)	superior
tri	(three)	tricycle
sub	(under)	submarine
post	(after)	postscript
ab	(from)	abnormal
trans	(across)	translate
em	(in)	embark
de	(from)	depart
inter	(between)	interurban
pro	(in front of)	promote
ex	(out of or out)	explain
en	(in)	enter
ob	(against)	object
per	(fully, through)	perfect

B. Phonic analysis
1. Knows phonic skills
   a. Single consonants and blends
   b. Short and long vowels
   c. Vowel teams:

ee ___	au ___	oi ___
ea ___	aw ___	oy ___
ai ___	oa ___	ou ___
ay ___	oo ___	ow ___

2. Knows vowel rules
   a. In attacking a vowel sound try first the short sound; if the word then doesn't make sense try the long sound
   b. Vowels are usually short when they appear as single vowels and are followed by a consonant
   c. Vowels are usually given the long sound when they appear alone and are the last letters of a word
   d. When two vowels appear together in a word, the first vowel is long and the second is silent
   e. In short word containing two vowels where one of the vowels is a final e, the first vowel will have a long sound while the final e is silent

C. Uses dictionary and glossary
1. Alphabetical Order:
   a. Order of letters in alphabet
   b. Alphabetical arrangement of words
2. Knows to divide the dictionary to determine in which 1/3 or 1/4 the word may be found
3. Knows the meaning and use of the phonetic spelling that follows in parenthesis each word in the dictionary
4. Knows the use of the pronunciation key
5. Knows to select the meaning which fits best according to the context in which the word is used
6. Knows the meaning and use of guide words
7. Knows the meaning and use of the secondary accent mark

III. Comprehension:
A. Finding the main idea
1. Choosing title for material read
2. Can identify key words and topic sentences
3. Summarizing

B. Finding details
1. Finding specific information
2. Interpreting descriptive words and phrases
3. Selecting facts to remember
4. Selecting facts to support main idea
5. Using study guides, charts, outlines
6. Verifying answers
7. Arranging ideas in sequence

C. Creative reading
1. Able to interpret story ideas (generalize)
2. Able to see relationships
3. Able to identify the mood of a reading selection
4. Able to identify author's purpose
5. Able to identify character traits

D. Formal outlining
1. Form
   a. Main ideas (I, II, III)
   b. Subordinate ideas (A, B, C)
2. Talking from an outline

IV. Oral and Silent Reading:
A. Understands material at grade level
B. Eye-voice span of three words in oral reading

Group Summary Profile—Fourth Level

The following pages present a Group Summary Profile at the Fourth Level which you can use to record the progress of the entire class in mastering the specific reading skills at that level. This profile can assist you in identifying groups of students who need instruction in a particular skill as well as in assessing the strengths and achievement levels of individual students. The Group Profile may also be used in conferences with administrators to discuss the status of a particular class.

Name of Teacher: ______________________________

GROUP SUMMARY PROFILE

FOURTH LEVEL

Student Names

Student Names	I. VOCABULARY	A. Word recognition	1. Knows new words in content fields	2. Recognizes similarities of known words	a. Compound words	b. Root words	c. Suffixes, prefixes	d. Plurals	e. Hyphenated words	f. Contractions	3. Recognizes unusual characteristics of words	B. Word meaning	1. Develops ability in getting meaning from context	2. Uses new words in sentences to show meaning	3. Knows punctuation	a. Italics	b. Quotation marks

School: ______________________ Year: __________

c. Parenthesis
d. Exclamation marks
4. Use of map skills

C. **Review Dolch Words**

II. **WORD ATTACK SKILLS**

A. **Structural analysis**

1. Knows and applies rules for syllables
   a. Each syllable contains a vowel
   b. Suffixes and prefixes are syllables
   c. Root word is not divided
   d. Two consonants, first syllable ends with first consonant
   e. Single consonant, consonant begins second syllable
   f. Word ends in le preceded by consonant, consonant begins last syllable
   g. X goes with preceding vowel to form syllable
   h. Ck go with preceding vowel and end the syllable
2. Knows accent clues
   a. First syllable usually accented
   b. Beginning syllables de, re, be, in and a usually unaccented
   c. Endings that form syllables are usually unaccented
   d. Ck following a single vowel is accented
3. Knows suffixes and prefixes
   a. Suffixes
   b. Prefixes

B. **Phonic analysis**

1. Knows phonic skills
   a. Single consonants and blends
   b. Short and long vowels
   c. Vowel teams
2. Knows vowel rules
   a. Try short sound, then long sound
   b. Short when single vowels and followed by consonant
   c. Vowels long when alone and last letters of a word
   d. Two vowels together, first is long, second is silent
   e. Two vowels with final e, first vowel will be long

C. Uses dictionary and glossary

1. Alphabetical order
   - a. Order of letters in alphabet
   - b. Alphabetical arrangement of words
2. Knows to divide the dictionary
3. Knows the meaning and use of the phonetic spelling in the dictionary
4. Knows the use of the pronunciation key
5. Knows to select the meaning which fits best according to the context in which the word is used
6. Knows the meaning and use of guide words
7. Knows the meaning and use of the secondary accent mark

III. COMPREHENSION

A. Finding the main idea

1. Choosing title for material read
2. Can identify key words and topic sentences
3. Summarizing

B. Finding details

1. Finding specific information
2. Interpreting descriptive words and phrases
3. Selecting facts to remember
4. Selecting facts to support main idea
5. Using study guides, charts, outlines
6. Verifying answers
7. Arranging ideas in sequence

C. Creative reading

1. Able to interpret story ideas (generalize)
2. Able to see relationships
3. Able to identify the mood of a reading selection
4. Able to identify author's purpose
5. Able to identify character traits

D. Formal outlining

1. Form
   - a. Main ideas
   - b. Subordinate ideas
2. Talking from an outline

IV. ORAL AND SILENT READING

A. Understands material at grade level

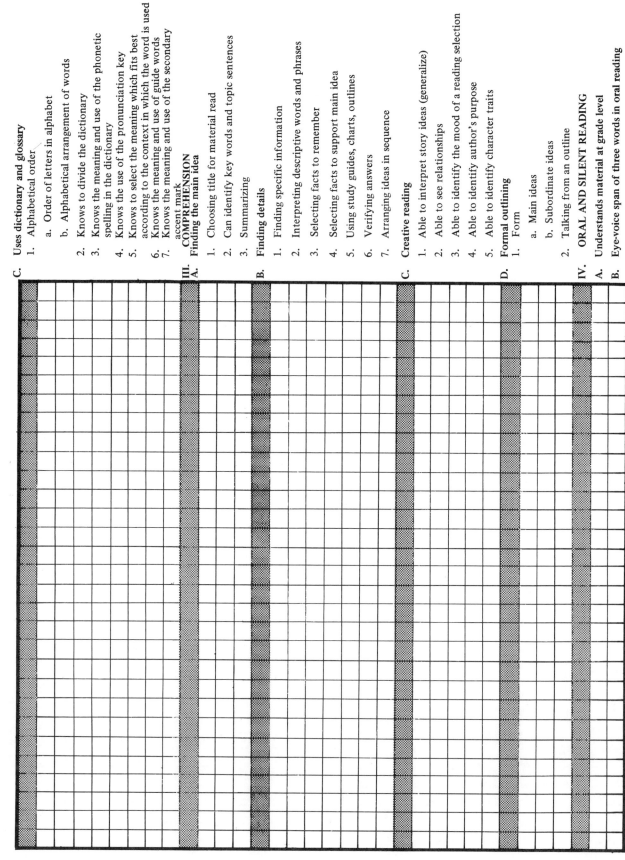

B. Eye-voice span of three words in oral reading

Reading Skills Competency Tests Fourth Level

Henriette L. Allen, Ph.D.

The test items which follow are written to measure the reading skills on the "Barbe Reading Skills Check List–Fourth Level."

The Competency Tests and Check List provide for:

- a quick, informal assessment of a student's competence in reading skills
- diagnosis and prescription of specific reading skill weaknesses and needs
- devising of appropriate teaching strategies for individuals and small or large groups
- continuous evaluation of each student's progress in the basic reading skills
- flexibility in planning the reading instructional program
- immediate feedback to the student and the teacher

The tests are designed to give you an efficient, systematic means to identify the specific reading skills needs of students.

FOURTH LEVEL

I. VOCABULARY   A. Word Recognition   1. Knows new words in content fields

OBJECTIVE: The pupil will demonstrate the ability to classify words into content areas.

DIRECTIONS: Read the following words carefully. Then write each word under the correct heading.

digit	centimeter	bacteria
hydrogen	pronoun	compass
library	energy	humus
chemical	diameter	subject
adjective	molecules	angle
fungi	words	evaporation
bar graph	vowel	speller
sentence	radius	quotient

	MATHEMATICS		LANGUAGE ARTS		SCIENCE
1.	digit	1.	library	1.	fungi
2.	bar graph	2.	adjective	2.	bacteria
3.	centimeter	3.	sentence	3.	hydrogen
4.	diameter	4.	pronoun	4.	molecules
5.	radius	5.	vowel	5.	evaporation
6.	compass	6.	speller	6.	energy
7.	angle	7.	subject	7.	chemical
8.	quotient	8.	words	8.	humus

MASTERY REQUIREMENT: 20 correct responses

Indicate mastery on the student response sheet with a check.

FOURTH LEVEL

I. VOCABULARY

Name ______________________________

A. Word Recognition

Date ______________________________

1. Knows new words in content fields

Mastery ___________

DIRECTIONS: Read the following words carefully. Then write each word under the correct heading.

digit	centimeter	bacteria
hydrogen	pronoun	compass
library	energy	humus
chemical	diameter	subject
adjective	molecules	angle
fungi	words	evaporation
bar graph	vowel	speller
sentence	radius	quotient

MATHEMATICS	LANGUAGE ARTS	SCIENCE
1. ____________	1. ____________	1. ____________
2. ____________	2. ____________	2. ____________
3. ____________	3. ____________	3. ____________
4. ____________	4. ____________	4. ____________
5. ____________	5. ____________	5. ____________
6. ____________	6. ____________	6. ____________
7. ____________	7. ____________	7. ____________
8. ____________	8. ____________	8 ____________

FOURTH LEVEL

I. VOCABULARY A. Word Recognition 1. Knows new words in content fields

OBJECTIVE: The pupil will demonstrate the ability to classify words into content areas.

DIRECTIONS: Read the following words carefully. Then write each word under the correct heading.

roses	coat	tent	soccer ball
trousers	azalea	daisies	shoes
net	cook stove	sleeping bag	zinnias
jacket	bat	scarf	glove
gardenia	insect repellent	knee pads	shirt
tennis racket	socks	mittens	flashlight
matches	canteen	carnations	violets
helmet	magnolia	cooking utensils	cleats

FLOWERS	ARTICLES OF CLOTHING	CAMPING EQUIPMENT	SPORTS EQUIPMENT
violets	shoes	tent	bat
roses	coat	sleeping bag	soccer ball
daisies	shirt	flashlight	tennis racket
carnations	jacket	cook stove	net
azalea	socks	canteen	glove
magnolia	scarf	inspect repellent	knee pads
zinnias	mittens	matches	helmet
gardenia	trousers	cooking utensils	cleats

MASTERY REQUIREMENT: 24 correct responses

Indicate mastery on the student response sheet with a check.

FOURTH LEVEL

I. VOCABULARY

A. Word Recognition

1. Knows new words in content fields

Name ______________________

Date ______________________

Mastery ________

DIRECTIONS: Read the following words carefully. Then write each word under the correct heading.

roses	coat	tent	soccer ball
trousers	azalea	daisies	shoes
net	cook stove	sleeping bag	zinnias
jacket	bat	scarf	glove
gardenia	insect repellent	knee pads	shirt
tennis racket	socks	mittens	flashlight
matches	canteen	carnations	violets
helmet	magnolia	cooking utensils	cleats

FLOWERS	ARTICLES OF CLOTHING	CAMPING EQUIPMENT	SPORTS EQUIPMENT
________	________	________	________
________	________	________	________
________	________	________	________
________	________	________	________
________	________	________	________
________	________	________	________
________	________	________	________
________	________	________	________

FOURTH LEVEL

I. VOCABULARY A. Word Recognition 2. Recognizes similarities of known words

a. Compound words

OBJECTIVE: The pupil will demonstrate the ability to recognize compound words.

DIRECTIONS: Read the following words and place an X in the front of the compound words.

X	1.	watermelon	X	7.	barefoot
____	2.	summer	____	8.	singer
X	3.	footprint	X	9.	basketball
X	4.	rainbow	X	10.	popcorn
X	5.	upstart	X	11.	runway
X	6.	goldfish	X	12.	sundial

MASTERY REQUIREMENT: Identifies 10 compound words

Indicate mastery on the student response sheet with a check.

FOURTH LEVEL

I. VOCABULARY

A. Word Recognition

2. Recognizes similarities of known words

a. Compound words

Name ____________________

Date ____________________

Mastery __________

DIRECTIONS: Read the following words and place an X in the front of the compound words.

________ 1. watermelon	________ 7. barefoot
________ 2. summer	________ 8. singer
________ 3. footprint	________ 9. basketball
________ 4. rainbow	________ 10. popcorn
________ 5. upstart	________ 11. runway
________ 6. goldfish	________ 12. sundial

FOURTH LEVEL

I. VOCABULARY A. Word Recognition 2. Recognizes similiarities of known words

b. Root words

OBJECTIVE: The pupil will demonstrate the ability to recognize root words.

DIRECTIONS: Read the following words carefully. Underline the root portion of the word.

1. golden
2. sulky
3. utterly
4. streaking
5. scornful
6. diplomats
7. musky
8. rapids
9. rarely
10. prehistoric
11. inheriting
12. impish

MASTERY REQUIREMENT: 10 correct responses

Indicate mastery on the student response sheet with a check.

FOURTH LEVEL

I. VOCABULARY

A. Word Recognition

2. Recognizes similarities of known words

b. Root words

Name ____________________

Date ____________________

Mastery __________

DIRECTIONS: Read the following words carefully. Underline the root portion of the word.

1. golden
2. sulky
3. utterly
4. streaking
5. scornful
6. diplomats
7. musky
8. rapids
9. rarely
10. prehistoric
11. inheriting
12. impish

FOURTH LEVEL

I. VOCABULARY A. Word Recognition 2. Recognizes similarities of known words

c. Suffixes and prefixes

OBJECTIVE: The pupil will demonstrate the ability to recognize prefixes and suffixes.

DIRECTIONS: Read the following words carefully. Write the prefix, root word and/or suffix in the correct column.

	PREFIX	ROOT WORD	SUFFIX
Ex. telephone	tele	phone	
1. mistake	mis	take	
2. helpful		help	ful
3. pretest	pre	test	
4. reluctantly		reluctant	ly
5. collection		collect	ion
6. berate	be	rate	
7. tricking		trick	ing
8. explore	ex	plore	
9. harshly		harsh	ly
10. submerge	sub	merge	

MASTERY REQUIREMENT: 8 correct responses

Indicate mastery on the student response sheet with a check.

FOURTH LEVEL

I. VOCABULARY

A. Word Recognition

2. Recognizes similarities of known words

c. Suffixes and prefixes

Name ____________________

Date ____________________

Mastery __________

DIRECTIONS: Read the following words carefully. Write the prefix, root word, and/or suffix in the correct column.

	PREFIX	ROOT WORD	SUFFIX
Ex. telephone	tele	phone	______
1. mistake	______	______	______
2. helpful	______	______	______
3. pretest	______	______	______
4. reluctantly	______	______	______
5. collection	______	______	______
6. berate	______	______	______
7. tricking	______	______	______
8. explore	______	______	______
9. harshly	______	______	______
10. submerge	______	______	______

FOURTH LEVEL

I. VOCABULARY **A. Word Recognition** **2. Recognizes similarities of known words**

d. Plurals

OBJECTIVE: The pupil will demonstrate the ability to change words from singular form to the plural.

DIRECTIONS: Read the following words carefully. On the line to the right of each word, write the plural form of the word.

1. skate	skates
2. switch	switches
3. friend	friends
4. dress	dresses
5. poppy	poppies
6. potato	potatoes
7. berry	berries
8. laundry	laundries
9. plane	planes
10. church	churches

MASTERY REQUIREMENT: 8 correct responses

Indicate mastery on the student response sheet with a check.

FOURTH LEVEL

I. VOCABULARY

A. Word Recognition

2. Recognizes similarities of known words

d. Plurals

Name ______________________

Date ______________________

Mastery __________

DIRECTIONS: Read the following words carefully. On the line to the right of each word, write the plural form of the word.

1. skate ____________________
2. switch ____________________
3. friend ____________________
4. dress ____________________
5. poppy ____________________
6. potato ____________________
7. berry ____________________
8. laundry ____________________
9. plane ____________________
10. church ____________________

FOURTH LEVEL

I. VOCABULARY A. Word Recognition 2. Recognizes similarities of known words

e. Hyphenated words

OBJECTIVE: The pupil will demonstrate the ability to recognize hyphenated words.

DIRECTIONS: Read the following words carefully. Place and X in front of the hyphenated words and an 0 in front of the words that are not hyphenated.

__X__ 1. standard - bearer

__0__ 2. bar graph

__0__ 3. peanut butter

__X__ 4. good - sized

__X__ 5. meat - eater

__X__ 6. in - between

__0__ 7. prenuclear

__X__ 8. merry - go - round

__X__ 9. forty - niner

__0__ 10. sea level

MASTERY REQUIREMENT: 8 correct responses

Indicate mastery on the student response sheet with a check.

FOURTH LEVEL

I. VOCABULARY

A. Word Recognition

2. Recognizes similarities of known words

e. Hyphenated words

Name ______________________

Date ______________________

Mastery ___________

DIRECTIONS: Read the following words carefully. Place and X in front of the hyphenated words and an 0 in front of the words that are not hyphenated.

_________ 1. standard - bearer

_________ 2. bar graph

_________ 3. peanut butter

_________ 4. good - sized

_________ 5. meat - eater

_________ 6. in - between

_________ 7. prenuclear

_________ 8. merry - go - round

_________ 9. forty - niner

_________ 10. sea level

FOURTH LEVEL

I. VOCABULARY A. Word Recognition 2. Recognizes similarities of known words

f. Contractions

OBJECTIVE: The pupil will demonstrate the ability to form contractions and to draw from a contraction the set of two words from which the contraction was formed.

DIRECTIONS: Write the contraction for the two words listed below.

1. did not	didn't
2. I am	I'm
3. are not	aren't
4. she is	she's
5. did not	didn't
6. could not	couldn't
7. it is	it's
8. he is	he's
9. I have	I've
10. there is	there's

PART II:

DIRECTIONS: Write the two words that form the contraction.

1. wouldn't	would not
2. can't	can not
3. here's	here is
4. you'll	you will
5. didn't	did not
6. don't	do not
7. she'll	she will
8. we're	we are
9. hadn't	had not
10. I'll	I will

MASTERY REQUIREMENT: 8 correct responses in each part

Indicate mastery on the student response sheet with a check.

FOURTH LEVEL

I. VOCABULARY

A. Word Recognition

2. Recognizes similarities of known words

f. Contractions

Name ______________________________

Date ______________________________

Mastery ___________

DIRECTIONS: Write the contraction for the two words listed below.

1. did not ____________________
2. I am ____________________
3. are not ____________________
4. she is ____________________
5. did not ____________________
6. could not ____________________
7. it is ____________________
8. he is ____________________
9. I have ____________________
10. there is ____________________

PART II:

DIRECTIONS: Write the two words that form the contraction.

1. wouldn't ____________________
2. can't ____________________
3. here's ____________________
4. you'll ____________________
5. didn't ____________________
6. don't ____________________
7. she'll ____________________
8. we're ____________________
9. hadn't ____________________
10. I'll ____________________

FOURTH LEVEL

I. VOCABULARY **A. Word Recognition** **3. Recognizes unusual characteristics of words**

OBJECTIVE: The pupil will demonstrate the ability to recognize unusual characteristics of words.

DIRECTIONS: Read the following words carefully. Write sentences using the words correctly.

1. hour ______________________

   our ______________________

2. know ______________________

   no ______________________

3. flour ______________________

   flower ______________________

4. where ______________________

   wear ______________________

5. which ______________________

   witch ______________________

MASTERY REQUIREMENT: 8 sentences using the words correctly

Indicate mastery on the student response sheet with a check.

FOURTH LEVEL

I. VOCABULARY

A. Word Recognition

3. Recognizes unusual characteristics of words

Name ____________________

Date ____________________

Mastery __________

DIRECTIONS: Read the following words carefully. Write sentences using the words correctly.

1. hour ____________________

   our ____________________

2. know ____________________

   no ____________________

3. flour ____________________

   flower ____________________

4. where ____________________

   wear ____________________

5. which ____________________

   witch ____________________

FOURTH LEVEL

I. VOCABULARY B. Word Meaning 1. Develops ability in getting meaning from context

OBJECTIVE: The pupil will demonstrate the ability to derive word meaning from the context of the sentence.

DIRECTIONS: Read the sentences carefully. Select the best word to complete the sentence and circle the word.

1. The price of the bow and ________________ was $6.95 at the sporting goods store.

   archer (arrow) airplane

2. Ferns grow in warm, moist places and many can be found in ________________.

   lakes ponds (swamps)

3. The airport was crowded with ________________ who were arriving to visit the United States for the first time.

   pilots navigators (tourists)

4. A heavenly body that revolves around a planet like the moon revolves around the earth is called a ________________.

   star (satellite) constellation

5. Nyette walked like a queen and this ________________ poise deceived many people.

   sloven slouched (regal)

6. The growth around the mouth of the fish that looks like a cat's whiskers gave the ________________ its name.

   (catfish) bass perch

7. The cat perched over the ________________ hoping to catch a goldfish.

   pen bowl (aquarium)

8. The science that deals with the study of the sun, moon, planets, and stars is called ________________.

   geology ecology (astronomy)

9. The umpire called the third strike and the ________________ was out.

   pitcher (batter) catcher

10. Eggs, flour, milk, and shortening are the ________________ of my pancake recipe.

    (ingredients) objects things

MASTERY REQUIREMENT: 8 correct responses

Indicate mastery on the student response sheet with a check.

FOURTH LEVEL

I. VOCABULARY

B. Word Meaning

1. Develops ability in getting meaning from context

Name ______________________

Date ______________________

Mastery __________

DIRECTIONS: Read the sentences carefully. Select the best word to complete the sentence and circle the word.

1. The price of the bow and ______________ was $6.95 at the sporting goods store.

   archer   arrow   airplane

2. Ferns grow in warm, moist places and many can be found in ______________.

   lakes   ponds   swamps

3. The airport was crowded with ______________ who were arriving to visit the United States for the first time.

   pilots   navigators   tourists

4. A heavenly body that revolves around a planet like the moon revolves around the earth is called a ______________.

   star   satellite   constellation

5. Nyette walked like a queen and this ______________ poise deceived many people.

   sloven   slouched   regal

6. The growth around the mouth of the fish that looks like a cat's whiskers gave the ______________ its name.

   catfish   bass   perch

7. The cat perched over the ______________ hoping to catch a goldfish.

   pen   bowl   aquarium

8. The science that deals with the study of the sun, moon, planets, and stars is called ______________.

   geology   ecology   astronomy

9. The umpire called the third strike and the ______________ was out.

   pitcher   batter   catcher

10. Eggs, flour, milk, and shortening are the ______________ of my pancake recipe.

   ingredients   objects   things

FOURTH LEVEL

I. VOCABULARY B. Word Meaning 2. Uses new words in sentences to show meaning

OBJECTIVE: The pupil will demonstrate the ability to use words in sentences to show meaning.

DIRECTIONS: Read the ten sentences below carefully. Select the correct word for each sentence from the following words and write the word on the blank line.

reed	flock	cycle
catalog	gap-toothed	village
spring	rifle	toothbrush
miser	peddler	necklace

1. The Bedouin boy watched over the large ____flock____ of sheep.
2. The cool water from the ____spring____ was refreshing after the hike.
3. When a person has a wide space between the teeth, one is said to be ____gap-toothed____.
4. The college ____catalog____ gave the names and addresses of all the students attending summer classes.
5. The mountaineer was most comfortable when he had his hunting dog and ____rifle____ by his side.
6. The ____peddler____ unloaded his pack of pots, pans, pins, and calico fabric.
7. A change which occurs over and over in the same order is called a ____cycle____.
8. The people gathered in the ____village____ to hear the news that the messenger brought from the battlefield.
9. A ____toothbrush____ is used to brush your teeth, clean in hard to get to places, and dust delicate items.
10. Placed around the princess's neck was a priceless ____necklace____ of rubies and diamonds.

MASTERY REQUIREMENT: 8 correct responses

Indicate mastery on the student response sheet with a check.

FOURTH LEVEL

I. VOCABULARY

B. Word Meaning

2. Uses new words in sentences to show meaning

Name ____________________

Date ____________________

Mastery __________

DIRECTIONS: Read the ten sentences below carefully. Select the correct word for each sentence from the following words and write the word on the blank line.

reed	flock	cycle
catalog	gap-toothed	village
spring	rifle	toothbrush
miser	peddler	necklace

1. The Bedouin boy watched over the large ________________ of sheep.

2. The cool water from the ________________ was refreshing after the hike.

3. When a person has a wide space between the teeth, one is said to be ____________.

4. The college ________________ gave the names and addresses of all the students attending summer classes.

5. The mountaineer was most comfortable when he had his hunting dog and ________________ by his side.

6. The ________________ unloaded his pack of pots, pans, pins, and calico fabric.

7. A change which occurs over and over in the same order is called a _____________.

8. The people gathered in the ________________ to hear the news that the messenger brought from the battlefield.

9. A ________________ is used to brush your teeth, clean in hard to get to places, and dust delicate items.

10. Placed around the princess's neck was a priceless ________________ of rubies and diamonds.

FOURTH LEVEL

I. VOCABULARY B. Word Meaning 3. Knows punctuation a. Italics, quotation marks, parenthesis, and exclamation marks

OBJECTIVE: The pupil will demonstrate a knowledge of italics, quotation parks, parenthesis, and exclamation marks.

DIRECTIONS: Read the following information carefully. Identify and write the information under the proper category of punctuation.

style of type	exclamation point
shows loudness	quotation marks
enclose exact words spoken or written	used for explanation
shows strong feeling	used to emphasize words
parenthesis	

Italics	" "
1. style of type	1. quotation marks
2. used to emphasize words	2. enclose exact words spoken or written
3.	3.

( )	!
1. parenthesis	1. exclamation point
2. used for explanation	2. shows loudness
3.	3. shows strong feeling

MASTERY REQUIREMENT: 8 correct responses

Indicate mastery on the student response sheet with a check.

FOURTH LEVEL

I. VOCABULARY Name ____________________

B. Word Meaning

Date ____________________

3. Knows punctuation

a. Italics, quotation marks, parenthesis, and exclamation marks

Mastery __________

DIRECTIONS: Read the following information carefully. Identify and write the information under the proper category of punctuation.

style of type	exclamation point
shows loudness	quotation marks
enclose exact words spoken or written	used for explanation
shows strong feeling	used to emphasize words
parenthesis	

Italics

1. ____________________
2. ____________________
3. ____________________

" "

1. ____________________
2. ____________________
3. ____________________

( )

1. ____________________
2. ____________________
3. ____________________

!

1. ____________________
2. ____________________
3. ____________________

FOURTH LEVEL

I. VOCABULARY B. Word Meaning 4. Use of map skills

OBJECTIVE: The pupil will demonstrate mastery of basic map skills.

DIRECTIONS: Study the direction arrows and map carefully. Read each of the statements following the map and fill in the blank with the correct answer.

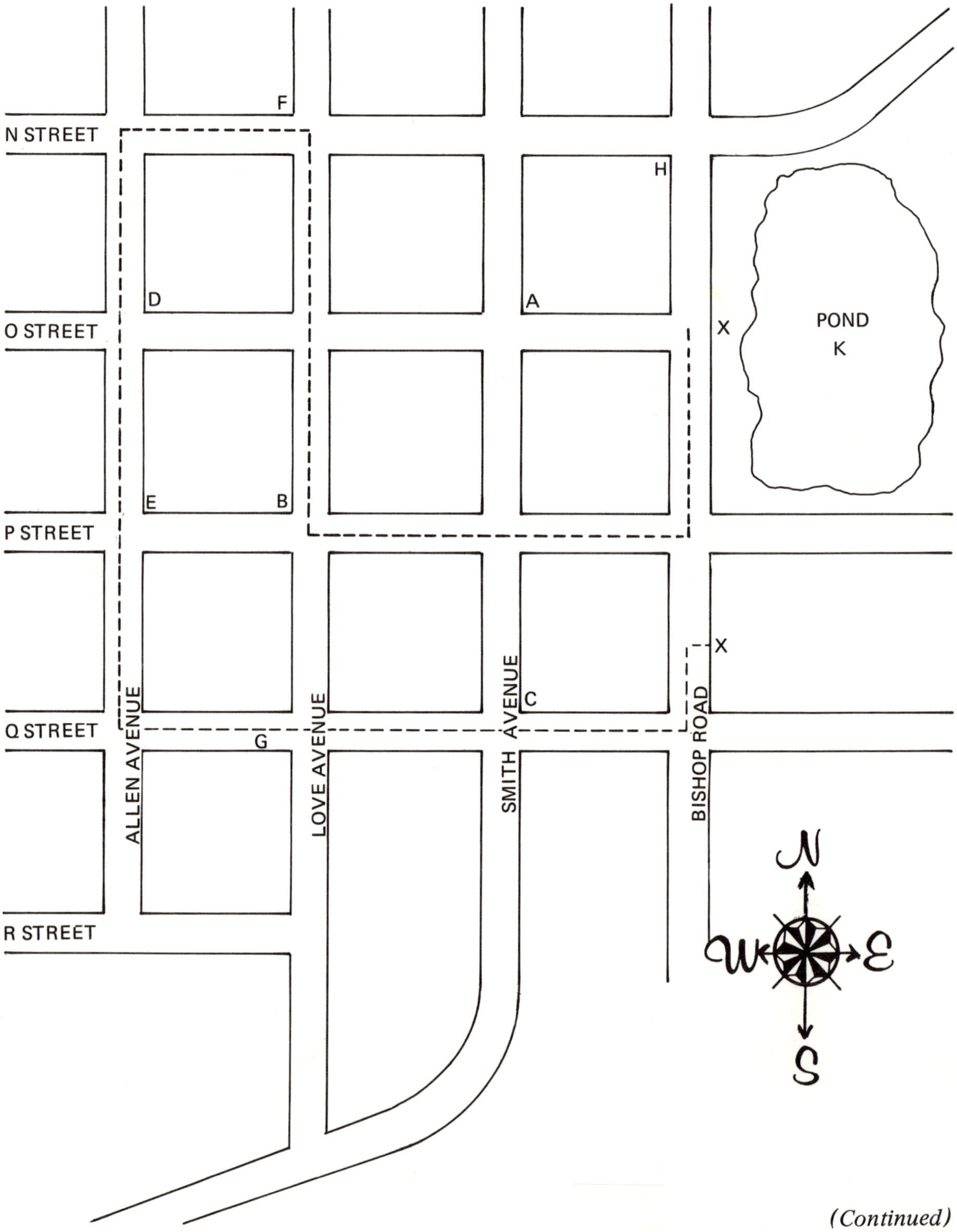

(Continued)

FOURTH LEVEL

I. VOCABULARY

B. Word Meaning

4. Use of map skills

Name ______________________________

Date ______________________________

Mastery ___________

DIRECTIONS: Study the direction arrows and map carefully. Read each of the statements following the map and fill in the blank with the correct answer.

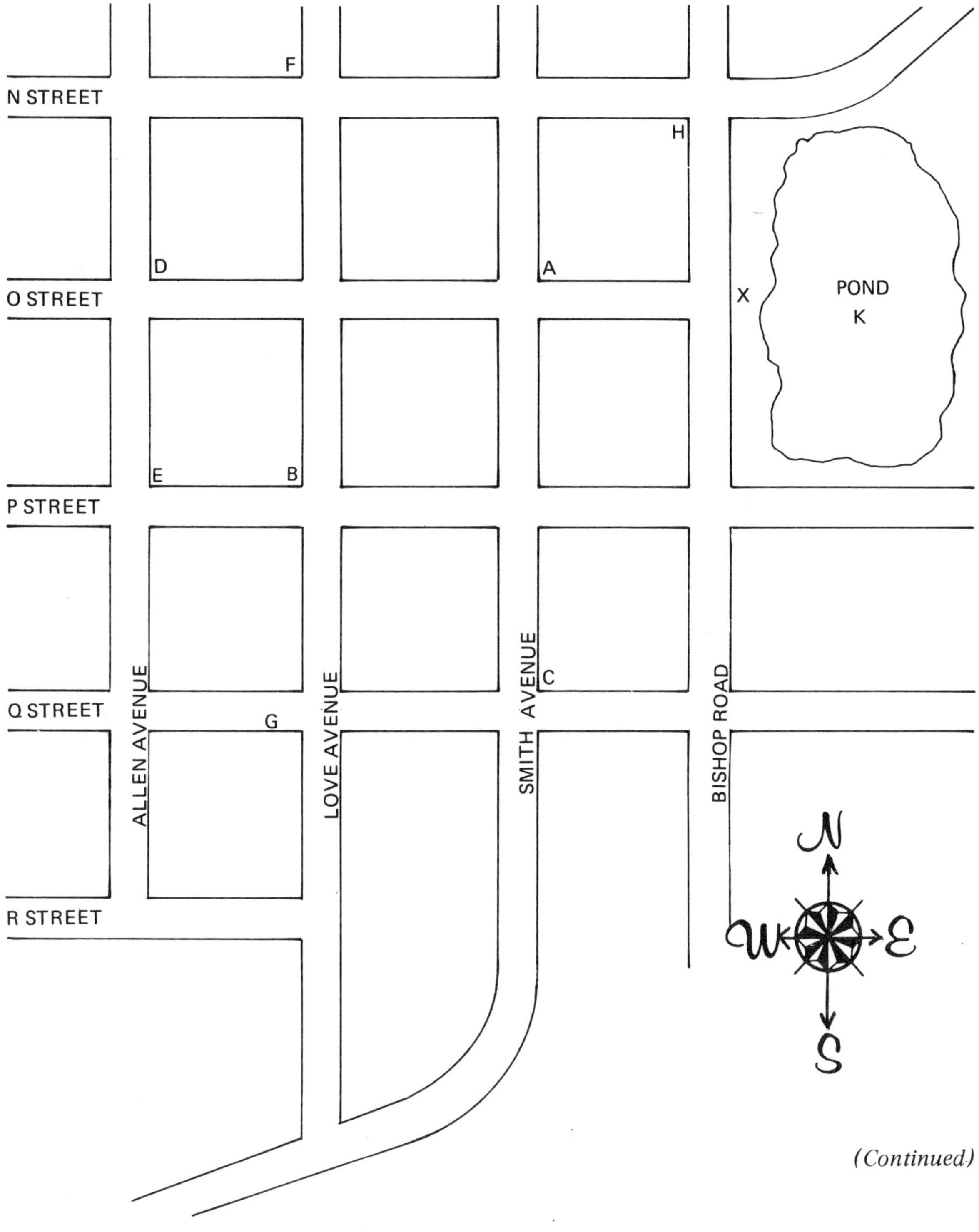

(Continued)

F 1. There is a bicycle shop at the northwest corner of Love Avenue and N Street.

C 2. Nyette lives on Smith Avenue where it crosses Q Street.

Allen Avenue 3. Which avenue dead ends into R Street?

A 4. Carlos has gone to visit Peter who lives one street north of P Street and two avenues east of Allen Avenue.

G 5. Margo was last seen riding her bicycle south on Love Avenue and turning west on Q Street.

N Street 6. Which street is east-west but bears north?

B 7. Grandma Mruk's house is two blocks west of the pond and one block south.

D 8. Ole Doc Lewis has an office on the northeast corner of Allen Avenue and O Street.

H 9. The mayor's house is on the southwest corner of Bishop Road and N Street.

E 10. Tony is visiting his uncle who lives on the northeast corner of Allen Avenue and P Street.

Love Avenue 11. Which north-south avenue flows into Smith Avenue?

O Street 12. Which east-west street ends at the pond?

Extra Take your pencil and draw on the map the route that Eddie took to go home after his fishing trip. He was at the pond. He went one block south and turned west for two blocks. Then he went north two blocks, west one block, south three blocks, east three blocks, north one-half block. Put an X where Eddie lives.

MASTERY REQUIREMENT: 10 correct responses

Indicate mastery on the student response sheet with a check.

__________ 1. There is a bicycle shop at the northwest corner of Love Avenue and N Street.

__________ 2. Nyette lives on Smith Avenue where it crosses Q Street.

__________ 3. Which avenue dead ends into R Street?

__________ 4. Carlos has gone to visit Peter who lives one street north of P Street and two avenues east of Allen Avenue.

__________ 5. Margo was last seen riding her bicycle south on Love Avenue and turning west on Q Street.

__________ 6. Which street is east-west but bears north?

__________ 7. Grandma Mruk's house is two blocks west of the pond and one block south.

__________ 8. Ole Doc Lewis has an office on the northeast corner of Allen Avenue and O Street.

__________ 9. The mayor's house is on the southwest corner of Bishop Road and N Street.

__________ 10. Tony is visiting his uncle who lives on the northeast corner of Allen Avenue and P Street.

__________ 11. Which north-south avenue flows into Smith Avenue?

__________ 12. Which east-west street ends at the pond?

Extra Take your pencil and draw on the map the route that Eddie took to go home after his fishing trip. He was at the pond. He went one block south and turned west for two blocks. Then he went north two blocks, west one block, south three blocks, east three blocks, north one-half block. Put an X where Eddie lives.

FOURTH LEVEL

I. VOCABULARY C. Review Dolch Words

OBJECTIVE: The pupil will recognize the 220 Dolch basic sight words.

DIRECTIONS: Read these words to the teacher, aide, or another pupil.

____ a	____ as	____ again	____ about	____ any
____ all	____ away	____ ate	____ after	____ better
____ am	____ be	____ but	____ always	____ both
____ an	____ black	____ cold	____ around	____ bring
____ and	____ brown	____ cut	____ ask	____ carry
____ are	____ by	____ fast	____ because	____ clean
____ at	____ came	____ first	____ been	____ could
____ big	____ did	____ five	____ before	____ done
____ blue	____ eat	____ fly	____ best	____ don't
____ call	____ fall	____ four	____ buy	____ draw
____ can	____ find	____ give	____ does	____ drink
____ come	____ for	____ goes	____ far	____ eight
____ do	____ from	____ going	____ found	____ every
____ down	____ get	____ got	____ full	____ hurt
____ funny	____ have	____ green	____ gave	____ know
____ go	____ her	____ had	____ grow	____ light
____ good	____ him	____ has	____ hold	____ myself
____ he	____ his	____ hot	____ how	____ never
____ help	____ if	____ its	____ just	____ own
____ here	____ into	____ long	____ keep	____ pick
____ I	____ laugh	____ made	____ kind	____ right
____ in	____ let	____ many	____ much	____ seven
____ is	____ live	____ new	____ must	____ shall
____ it	____ may	____ not	____ now	____ show
____ jump	____ my	____ of	____ off	____ their
____ like	____ no	____ open	____ once	____ them
____ little	____ old	____ or	____ only	____ then
____ look	____ on	____ our	____ round	____ there
____ make	____ one	____ please	____ sleep	____ these
____ me	____ over	____ pull	____ small	____ think
____ out	____ put	____ read	____ take	____ those
____ play	____ said	____ saw	____ tell	____ together
____ pretty	____ she	____ say	____ thank	____ use
____ ran	____ sit	____ sing	____ that	____ very
____ red	____ some	____ six	____ they	____ want
____ ride	____ stop	____ soon	____ this	____ warm
____ run	____ three	____ start	____ too	____ wash
____ see	____ today	____ ten	____ try	____ went
____ so	____ two	____ upon	____ under	____ what
____ the	____ was	____ us	____ walk	____ when
____ to	____ will	____ who	____ well	____ where
____ up	____ work	____ why	____ were	____ which
____ we	____ yes	____ wish	____ white	____ would
____ you	____ yellow	____ your	____ with	____ write

MASTERY REQUIREMENT: All correct

Indicate mastery on the student response sheet with a check.

FOURTH LEVEL

I. VOCABULARY

Name ______________________________

C. Review Dolch Words

Date ______________________________

Mastery ___________

DIRECTIONS: Read these words to the teacher, aide, or another pupil.

____ a	____ as	____ again	____ about	____ any
____ all	____ away	____ ate	____ after	____ better
____ am	____ be	____ but	____ always	____ both
____ an	____ black	____ cold	____ around	____ bring
____ and	____ brown	____ cut	____ ask	____ carry
____ are	____ by	____ fast	____ because	____ clean
____ at	____ came	____ first	____ been	____ could
____ big	____ did	____ five	____ before	____ done
____ blue	____ eat	____ fly	____ best	____ don't
____ call	____ fall	____ four	____ buy	____ draw
____ can	____ find	____ give	____ does	____ drink
____ come	____ for	____ goes	____ far	____ eight
____ do	____ from	____ going	____ found	____ every
____ down	____ get	____ got	____ full	____ hurt
____ funny	____ have	____ green	____ gave	____ know
____ go	____ her	____ had	____ grow	____ light
____ good	____ him	____ has	____ hold	____ myself
____ he	____ his	____ hot	____ how	____ never
____ help	____ if	____ its	____ just	____ own
____ here	____ into	____ long	____ keep	____ pick
____ I	____ laugh	____ made	____ kind	____ right
____ in	____ let	____ many	____ much	____ seven
____ is	____ live	____ new	____ must	____ shall
____ it	____ may	____ not	____ now	____ show
____ jump	____ my	____ of	____ off	____ their
____ like	____ no	____ open	____ once	____ them
____ little	____ old	____ or	____ only	____ then
____ look	____ on	____ our	____ round	____ there
____ make	____ one	____ please	____ sleep	____ these
____ me	____ over	____ pull	____ small	____ think
____ out	____ put	____ read	____ take	____ those
____ play	____ said	____ saw	____ tell	____ together
____ pretty	____ she	____ say	____ thank	____ use
____ ran	____ sit	____ sing	____ that	____ very
____ red	____ some	____ six	____ they	____ want
____ ride	____ stop	____ soon	____ this	____ warm
____ run	____ three	____ start	____ too	____ wash
____ see	____ today	____ ten	____ try	____ went
____ so	____ two	____ upon	____ under	____ what
____ the	____ was	____ us	____ walk	____ when
____ to	____ will	____ who	____ well	____ where
____ up	____ work	____ why	____ were	____ which
____ we	____ yes	____ wish	____ white	____ would
____ you	____ yellow	____ your	____ with	____ write

FOURTH LEVEL

II. WORD ATTACK SKILLS A. Structural Analysis 1. Knows rules for syllables

OBJECTIVE: The pupil will demonstrate a knowledge of the eight syllabication rules at the fourth level.

DIRECTIONS: Say each of the following words to yourself. Think carefully and then write the word correctly divided into syllables.

1. tangle	tan gle	11. iron	i ron
2. padre	pa dre	12. stockade	stock ade
3. oxford	ox ford	13. harbor	har bor
4. potion	po tion	14. oxbow	ox bow
5. omit	o mit	15. crusty	crust y
6. bangle	ban gle	16. blunder	blun der
7. morsel	mor sel	17. equal	e qual
8. flocking	flock ing	18. locker	lock er
9. safety	safe ty	19. disjoin	dis join
10. agent	a gent	20. wrangle	wran gle

MASTERY REQUIREMENT: 17 correct responses

Indicate mastery on the student response sheet with a check.

FOURTH LEVEL

II. WORD ATTACK SKILLS

A. Structural Analysis

1. Knows rules for syllables

Name ______________________________

Date ______________________________

Mastery ___________

DIRECTIONS: Say each of the following words to yourself. Think carefully and then write the word correctly divided into syllables.

1. tangle	______________	11. iron	______________
2. padre	______________	12. stockade	______________
3. oxford	______________	13. harbor	______________
4. potion	______________	14. oxbow	______________
5. omit	______________	15. crusty	______________
6. bangle	______________	16. blunder	______________
7. morsel	______________	17. equal	______________
8. flocking	______________	18. locker	______________
9. safety	______________	19. disjoin	______________
10. agent	______________	20. wrangle	______________

FOURTH LEVEL

II. WORD ATTACK SKILLS A. Structural Analysis 1. Knows and applies rules for syllables

a. Each syllable must contain a vowel and a single vowel can be a syllable

OBJECTIVE: The pupil will demonstrate a knowledge of syllabication whereby each syllable must have a vowel and a single vowel can be a syllable.

DIRECTIONS: Read the following words to yourself. Write the number of syllables in each word on the line next to the word.

1. cub	1	11. roam	1
2. ad	1	12. tie	1
3. fifty	2	13. cracker	2
4. sort	1	14. oak	1
5. raft	1	15. hammer	2
6. coffee	2	16. sidewalk	2
7. oxen	2	17. toothpick	2
8. so	1	18. net	1
9. oil	1	19. rumble	2
10. magic	2	20. sky	1

MASTERY REQUIREMENT: 16 correct responses

Indicate mastery on the student response sheet with a check.

FOURTH LEVEL

II. WORD ATTACK SKILLS

Name ______________________

A. Structural Analysis

Date ______________________

1. Knows and applies rules for syllables

Mastery __________

a. Each syllable must contain a vowel and a single vowel can be a syllable

DIRECTIONS: Read the following words to yourself. Write the number of syllables in each word on the line next to the word.

1.	cub	________	11.	roam	________
2.	ad	________	12.	tie	________
3.	fifty	________	13.	cracker	________
4.	sort	________	14.	oak	________
5.	raft	________	15.	hammer	________
6.	coffee	________	16.	sidewalk	________
7.	oxen	________	17.	toothpick	________
8.	so	________	18.	net	________
9.	oil	________	19.	rumble	________
10.	magic	________	20.	sky	________

FOURTH LEVEL

II. WORD ATTACK SKILLS A. Structural Analysis 1. Knows and applies rules for syllables

b. Suffixes and prefixes are syllables with meanings of their own

OBJECTIVE: The pupil will demonstrate knowledge of the syllabication rule that suffixes and prefixes are syllables.

DIRECTIONS: Say each of the following words to yourself. Write the word divided into syllables on the blank line beside the word.

1. kindness	kind ness
2. preserve	pre serve
3. berate	be rate
4. return	re turn
5. measure	meas ure
6. player	play er
7. seventy	seven ty
8. expose	ex pose
9. luggage	lug gage
10. inform	in form

MASTERY REQUIREMENT: 8 correct responses

Indicate mastery on the student response sheet with a check.

FOURTH LEVEL

II. WORD ATTACK SKILLS

A. Structural Analysis

1. Knows and applies rules for syllables

b. Suffixes and prefixes are syllables with meanings of their own

Name ______________________________

Date ______________________________

Mastery __________

DIRECTIONS: Say each of the following words to yourself. Write the word divided into syllables on the blank line beside the word.

1. kindness ____________________
2. preserve ____________________
3. berate ____________________
4. return ____________________
5. measure ____________________
6. player ____________________
7. seventy ____________________
8. expose ____________________
9. luggage ____________________
10. inform ____________________

FOURTH LEVEL

II. WORD ATTACK SKILLS **A. Structural Analysis** **1. Knows and applies rules for syllables**

c. The root word is not divided

OBJECTIVE: The pupil will demonstrate an understanding of the syllabication rules that the root word is a syllable and is not divided.

DIRECTIONS: Read each of the words on the left carefully. Circle the word that is correctly divided into syllables.

1. deeply	a) deep ly	b) de eply	c) deepl y	d) dee ply
2. invite	a) inv ite	b) i nvite	c) in vite	d) invi te
3. flashing	a) fla shing	b) flas hing	c) flashi ng	d) flash ing
4. displease	a) di splease	b) disp lease	c) displ ease	d) dis please
5. buzzing	a) buzz ing	b) buz zing	c) bu zzing	d) buzzi ng
6. coolness	a) co olness	b) cooln ess	c) cool ness	d) coo lness
7. costly	a) cos tly	b) cost ly	c) co stly	d) costl y
8. disclaim	a) dis claim	b) di sclaim	c) discl aim	d) disc laim
9. present	a) pres ent	b) pr esent	c) pre sent	d) prese nt
10. shorter	a) sho rter	b) shor ter	c) shorte r	d) short er

MASTERY REQUIREMENT: 8 correct responses

Indicate mastery on the student response sheet with a check.

FOURTH LEVEL

II. WORD ATTACK SKILLS

Name ____________________

A. Structural Analysis

Date ____________________

1. Knows and applies rules for syllables

Mastery __________

c. The root word is not divided

DIRECTIONS: Read each of the words on the left carefully. Circle the word that is correctly divided into syllables.

1.	deeply	a) deep ly	b) de eply	c) deepl y	d) dee ply
2.	invite	a) inv ite	b) i nvite	c) in vite	d) invi te
3.	flashing	a) fla shing	b) flas hing	c) flashi ng	d) flash ing
4.	displease	a) di splease	b) disp lease	c) displ ease	d) dis please
5.	buzzing	a) buzz ing	b) buz zing	c) bu zzing	d) buzzi ng
6.	coolness	a) co olness	b) cooln ess	c) cool ness	d) coo lness
7.	costly	a) cos tly	b) cost ly	c) co stly	d) costl y
8.	disclaim	a) dis claim	b) di sclaim	c) discl aim	d) disc laim
9.	present	a) pres ent	b) pr esent	c) pre sent	d) prese nt
10.	shorter	a) sho rter	b) shor ter	c) shorte r	d) short er

FOURTH LEVEL

II. WORD ATTACK SKILLS A. Structural Analysis 1. Knows and applies rules for syllables

d. If the first vowel is followed by two consonants, the first syllable usually ends with the first consonant

OBJECTIVE: The pupil will demonstrate knowledge of the syllable rule that if the first vowel is followed by two consonants, the first syllable usually ends with the first consonant.

DIRECTIONS: Read each numbered word to yourself. Then fill in the circle in front of the correct syllabication of the word.

1. dorsal
   - ○ a. do rsal
   - ○ b. dors al
   - ○ c. dorsal
   - ● d. dor sal

2. foppish
   - ● a. fop pish
   - ○ b. fo ppish
   - ○ c. fopp ish
   - ○ d. foppi sh

3. whimper
   - ○ a. whi mper
   - ● b. whim per
   - ○ c. whimp er
   - ○ d. whimper

4. effect
   - ○ a. e ffect
   - ● b. ef fect
   - ○ c. eff ect
   - ○ d. effe ct

5. burdock
   - ○ a. bu rdock
   - ○ b. burd ock
   - ● c. bur dock
   - ○ d. burdo ck

6. antic
   - ● a. an tic
   - ○ b. a ntic
   - ○ c. ant ic
   - ○ d. anti c

7. altar
   - ○ a. a ltar
   - ○ b. alt ar
   - ○ c. altar
   - ● d. al tar

8. carcass
   - ○ a. ca rcass
   - ● b. car cass
   - ○ c. c arcass
   - ○ d. carca ss

9. convert
   - ● a. con vert
   - ○ b. conv ert
   - ○ c. co nvert
   - ○ d. conve rt

10. wallow
   - ○ a. wall ow
   - ○ b. wa llow
   - ● c. wal low
   - ○ d. wallo w

MASTERY REQUIREMENT: 8 correct responses

Indicate mastery on the student response sheet with a check.

FOURTH LEVEL

II. WORD ATTACK SKILLS

Name ______________________________

A. Structural Analysis

Date ______________________________

1. Knows and applies rules for syllables

Mastery __________

d. If the first vowel is followed by two consonants, the first syllable usually ends with the first consonant

DIRECTIONS: Read each numbered word to yourself. Then fill in the circle in front of the correct syllabication of the word.

1. dorsal
   - O a. do rsal
   - O b. dors al
   - O c. dorsal
   - O d. dor sal

2. foppish
   - O a. fop pish
   - O b. fo ppish
   - O c. fopp ish
   - O d. foppi sh

3. whimper
   - O a. whi mper
   - O b. whim per
   - O c. whimp er
   - O d. whimper

4. effect
   - O a. e ffect
   - O b. ef fect
   - O c. eff ect
   - O d. effe ct

5. burdock
   - O a. bu rdock
   - O b. burd ock
   - O c. bur dock
   - O d. burdo ck

6. antic
   - O a. an tic
   - O b. a ntic
   - O c. ant ic
   - O d. anti c

7. altar
   - O a. a ltar
   - O b. alt ar
   - O c. altar
   - O d. al tar

8. carcass
   - O a. ca rcass
   - O b. car cass
   - O c. c arcass
   - O d. carca ss

9. convert
   - O a. con vert
   - O b. conv ert
   - O c. co nvert
   - O d. conve rt

10. wallow
   - O a. wall ow
   - O b. wa llow
   - O c. wal low
   - O d. wallo w

FOURTH LEVEL

II. WORD ATTACK SKILLS A. Structural Analysis 1. Knows and applies rules for syllables

e. If the first vowel is followed by a single consonant, the consonant usually begins the second syllable

OBJECTIVE: The pupil will demonstrate an understanding of the syllable rule that if the first vowel is followed by a single consonant, the consonant usually begins the second syllable.

DIRECTIONS: Read each of the words on the left carefully. Circle the word that is correctly divided into syllables in the line to the right.

1. cubic	a) cu bic	b) cub ic	c) cubic	d) cubi c
2. humor	a) hum or	b) humo r	c) hu mor	d) humor
3. prefix	a) pref ix	b) pre fix	c) pr efix	d) prefix
4. drama	a) drama	b) dr ama	c) dram a	d) dra ma
5. behind	a) beh ind	b) be hind	c) behind	d) behi nd
6. flavor	a) fla vor	b) flav or	c) fl avor	d) flavor
7. spinal	a) spin al	b) sp inal	c) spi nal	d) spinal
8. student	a) stud ent	b) st udent	c) student	d) stu dent
9. event	a) e vent	b) ev ent	c) eve nt	d) event
10. bison	a) bis on	b) b ison	c) bi son	d) bison

MASTERY REQUIREMENT: 8 correct responses

Indicate mastery on the student response sheet with a check.

FOURTH LEVEL

II. WORD ATTACK SKILLS

A. Structural Analysis

1. Knows and applies rules for syllables

e. If the first vowel is followed by a single consonant, the consonant usually begins the second syllable

Name ____________________

Date ____________________

Mastery __________

DIRECTIONS: Read each of the words on the left carefully. Circle the word that is correctly divided into syllables in the line to the right.

1. cubic	a) cu bic	b) cub ic	c) cubic	d) cubi c
2. humor	a) hum or	b) humo r	c) hu mor	d) humor
3. prefix	a) pref ix	b) pre fix	c) pr efix	d) prefix
4. drama	a) drama	b) dr ama	c) dram a	d) dra ma
5. behind	a) beh ind	b) be hind	c) behind	d) behi nd
6. flavor	a) fla vor	b) flav or	c) fl avor	d) flavor
7. spinal	a) spin al	b) sp inal	c) spi nal	d) spinal
8. student	a) stud ent	b) st udent	c) student	d) stu dent
9. event	a) e vent	b) ev ent	c) eve nt	d) event
10. bison	a) bis on	b) b ison	c) bi son	d) bison

FOURTH LEVEL

II. WORD ATTACK SKILLS **A. Structural Analysis** **1. Knows and applies rules for syllables**

f. If a word ends in le preceded by a consonant, that consonant begins the last syllable

OBJECTIVE: The pupil will demonstrate an understanding of the syllable rule that if a word ends in le preceded by a consonant, that consonant begins the last syllable.

DIRECTIONS: Say each of the numbered words to yourself. Fill in the circle in front of the correct syllabication of the word.

1. fable
   - ● a. fa ble
   - ○ b. fab le
   - ○ c. fabl e
   - ○ d. fable

2. hurtle
   - ○ a. hurt le
   - ○ b. hu rtle
   - ● c. hur tle
   - ○ d. hurtle

3. tingle
   - ○ a. ting le
   - ● b. tin gle
   - ○ c. ti ngle
   - ○ d. tingle

4. brindle
   - ○ a. brind le
   - ○ b. bri ndle
   - ○ c. brindle
   - ● d. brin dle

5. cable
   - ● a. ca ble
   - ○ b. cab le
   - ○ c. cabl e
   - ○ d. cable

6. maple
   - ○ a. maple
   - ○ b. map le
   - ● c. ma ple
   - ○ d. mapl e

7. uncle
   - ○ a. unc le
   - ○ b. uncle
   - ○ c. u ncle
   - ● d. un cle

8. purple
   - ● a. pur ple
   - ○ b. purp le
   - ○ c. pu rple
   - ○ d. purple

9. whittle
   - ○ a. whi ttle
   - ○ b. whitt le
   - ● c. whit tle
   - ○ d. whittle

10. stable
    - ○ a. stab le
    - ● b. sta ble
    - ○ c. stabl e
    - ○ d. stable

MASTERY REQUIREMENT: 8 correct responses

Indicate mastery on the student response sheet with a check.

FOURTH LEVEL

II. WORD ATTACK SKILLS

A. Structural Analysis

1. Knows and applies rules for syllables

f. If a word ends in le preceded by a consonant, that consonant begins the last syllable.

Name ______________________

Date ______________________

Mastery __________

DIRECTIONS: Say each of the numbered words to yourself. Fill in the circle in front of the correct syllabication of the word.

1. fable
   - O a. fa ble
   - O b. fab le
   - O c. fabl e
   - O d. fable

2. hurtle
   - O a. hurt le
   - O b. hu rtle
   - O c. hur tle
   - O d. hurtle

3. tingle
   - O a. ting le
   - O b. tin gle
   - O c. ti ngle
   - O d. tingle

4. brindle
   - O a. brind le
   - O b. bri ndle
   - O c. brindle
   - O d. brin dle

5. cable
   - O a. ca ble
   - O b. cab le
   - O c. cabl e
   - O d. cable

6. maple
   - O a. maple
   - O b. map le
   - O c. ma ple
   - O d. mapl e

7. uncle
   - O a. unc le
   - O b. uncle
   - O c. u ncle
   - O d. un cle

8. purple
   - O a. pur ple
   - O b. purp le
   - O c. pu rple
   - O d. purple

9. whittle
   - O a. whi ttle
   - O b. whitt le
   - O c. whit tle
   - O d. whittle

10. stable
   - O a. stab le
   - O b. sta ble
   - O c. stabl e
   - O d. stable

FOURTH LEVEL

II. WORD ATTACK SKILLS A. Structural Analysis 1. Knows and applies rules for syllables

g. The letter x always goes with the preceding vowel to form a syllable

OBJECTIVE: The pupil will demonstrate a knowledge of the syllable rule that the letter x always goes with the preceding vowel to form a syllable.

DIRECTIONS: Write each of the following words in syllable form after you have carefully said the word to yourself.

1. axle	ax le
2. exam	ex am
3. exalt	ex alt
4. excess	ex cess
5. oxen	ox en
6. exceed	ex ceed
7. exit	ex it
8. excite	ex cite
9. axis	ax is
10. exact	ex act

MASTERY REQUIREMENT: 8 correct responses

Indicate mastery on the student response sheet with a check.

FOURTH LEVEL

II. WORD ATTACK SKILLS

Name ______________________

A. Structural Analysis

Date ______________________

1. Knows and applies rules for syllables

Mastery __________

g. The letter x always goes with the preceding vowel to form a syllable

DIRECTIONS: Write each of the following words in syllable form after you have carefully said the word to yourself.

1. axle ______________________

2. exam ______________________

3. exalt ______________________

4. excess ______________________

5. oxen ______________________

6. exceed ______________________

7. exit ______________________

8. excite ______________________

9. axis ______________________

10. exact ______________________

FOURTH LEVEL

II. WORD ATTACK SKILLS A. Structural Analysis 1. Knows and applies rules for syllables

h. The letters ck go with the preceding vowel and end the syllable

OBJECTIVE: The pupil will demonstrate an understanding of the syllable rule that the letters ck go with the preceding vowel and end the syllable.

DIRECTIONS: Say each of the following words to yourself. Circle the correct syllabication of the word in Column A or Column B.

	Column A	*Column B*
1. pickle	(pick le)	pic kle
2. chicken	chic ken	(chick en)
3. socket	soc ket	(sock et)
4. stocking	(stock ing)	stoc king
5. locket	(lock et)	loc ket
6. nickel	nic kel	(nick el)
7. pocket	(pock et)	poc ket
8. flocking	floc king	(flock ing)
9. sprocket	sproc ket	(sprock et)
10. fickle	(fick le)	fic kle

MASTERY REQUIREMENT: 8 correct responses

Indicate mastery on the student response sheet with a check.

FOURTH LEVEL

II. WORD ATTACK SKILLS

A. Structural Analysis

1. Knows and applies rules for syllables

h. The letters ck go with the preceding vowel and end the syllable

Name ______________________________

Date ______________________________

Mastery ___________

DIRECTIONS: Say each of the following words to yourself. Circle the correct syllabication of the word in Column A or Column B.

	Column A	*Column B*
1. pickle	pick le	pic kle
2. chicken	chic ken	chick en
3. socket	soc ket	sock et
4. stocking	stock ing	stoc king
5. locket	lock et	loc ket
6. nickel	nic kel	nick el
7. pocket	pock et	poc ket
8. flocking	floc king	flock ing
9. sprocket	sproc ket	sprock et
10. fickle	fick le	fic kle

FOURTH LEVEL

II. WORD ATTACK SKILLS A. Structural Analysis 2. Knows accent clues

OBJECTIVE: The pupil will demonstrate an understanding of the four accent rules of the fourth level.

DIRECTIONS: Read each of the following words to yourself. Think carefully and place the accent mark on the correct syllable of the word in the second row.

1. incite	in cite´
2. calling	call´ ing
3. kicker	kick´ er
4. despise	de spise´
5. ocean	o´ cean
6. madly	mad´ ly
7. repel	re pel´
8. luckless	luck´ less
9. coolness	cool´ ness
10. empty	emp´ ty
11. ahead	a head´
12. pucker	puck´ er
13. lowly	low´ ly
14. invent	in vent´
15. cracker	crack´ er
16. shyly	shy´ ly
17. idol	i´ dol
18. beyond	be yond´
19. stacking	stack´ ing
20. silly	sil´ ly

MASTERY REQUIREMENT: 16 correct responses

Indicate mastery on the student response sheet with a check.

FOURTH LEVEL

II. WORD ATTACK SKILLS

A. Structural Analysis

2. Knows accent rules

Name ______________________

Date ______________________

Mastery __________

DIRECTIONS: Read each of the following words to yourself. Think carefully and place the accent mark on the correct syllable of the word in the second row.

1. incite	in cite
2. calling	call ing
3. kicker	kick er
4. despise	de spise
5. ocean	o cean
6. madly	mad ly
7. repel	re pel
8. luckless	luck less
9. coolness	cool ness
10. empty	emp ty
11. ahead	a head
12. pucker	puck er
13. lowly	low ly
14. invent	in vent
15. cracker	crack er
16. shyly	shy ly
17. idol	i dol
18. beyond	be yond
19. stacking	stack ing
20. silly	sil ly

FOURTH LEVEL

II. WORD ATTACK SKILLS A. Structural Analysis 2. Knows accent clues

a. The first syllable is usually accented unless it is a prefix

OBJECTIVE: The pupil will demonstrate a knowledge of the accent rule that the first syllable in a word is usually accented unless it is a prefix.

DIRECTIONS: There are two words in each row. Say the words to yourself and place an X on the word that is correctly accented.

1.	re view´ X	care ful´
2.	broad cast´	bold´ er X
3.	clut ter´	weak´ ness X
4.	pre judge´ X	re´ sist
5.	un sung X	pre´ wash
6.	sun´ set X	scru ple´
7.	dis´ close	dis own´ X
8.	pro ceed X	out´ strip
9.	in´ vade	hood´ ed X
10.	gris´ tle X	gross ness´

MASTERY REQUIRMENT: 8 correct responses

Indicate mastery on the student response sheet with a check.

FOURTH LEVEL

II. WORD ATTACK SKILLS

A. Structural Analysis

2. Knows accent clues

a. The first syllable is usually accented unless it is a prefix

Name ______________________________

Date ______________________________

Mastery ___________

DIRECTIONS: There are two words in each row. Say the words to yourself and place an X on the word that is correctly accented.

1.	re view´	care ful´
2.	broad cast´	bold´ er
3.	clut ter´	weak´ ness
4.	pre judge´	re´ sist
5.	un sung´	pre´ wash
6.	sun´ set	scru ple´
7.	dis´ close	dis own´
8.	pro ceed´	out´ strip
9.	in´ vade	hood´ ed
10.	gris´ tle	gross ness´

FOURTH LEVEL

II. WORD ATTACK SKILLS A. Structural Analysis 2. Knows accent rules

b. Beginning syllables de, re, be, in and a are usually unaccented

OBJECTIVE: The pupil will demonstrate a knowledge of the accent rule that the beginning syllables de, re, be, in and a are usually unaccented.

DIRECTIONS: In each row draw a circle around the word in which the first syllable is not accented.

	Column A	*Column B*	*Column C*
1.	avid	(across)	atom
2.	(deform)	delta	dental
3.	beetle	beeline	(behold)
4.	relish	(report)	rental
5.	infant	intern	(intent)
6.	(adapt)	arrant	arrow
7.	(deter)	detour	devil
8.	aster	(alarm)	ashen
9.	(remake)	redden	recent
10.	bellow	(beneath)	belly

MASTERY REQUIREMENT: 8 correct responses

Indicate mastery on the student response sheet with a check.

FOURTH LEVEL

II. WORD ATTACK SKILLS

A. Structural Analysis

2. Knows accent rules

b. Beginning syllables de, re, be, in and a are usually unaccented

Name ______________________

Date ______________________

Mastery __________

DIRECTIONS: In each row draw a circle around the word in which the first syllable is not accented.

	Column A	*Column B*	*Column C*
1.	avid	across	atom
2.	deform	delta	dental
3.	beetle	beeline	behold
4.	relish	report	rental
5.	infant	intern	intent
6.	adapt	arrant	arrow
7.	deter	detour	devil
8.	aster	alarm	ashen
9.	remake	redden	recent
10.	bellow	beneath	belly

FOURTH LEVEL

II. WORD ATTACK SKILLS A. Structural Analysis 2. Knows accent rules

c. Endings that form syllables are usually unaccented

OBJECTIVE: The pupil will demonstrate an understanding of the accent rule that endings that form syllables are usually unaccented.

DIRECTIONS: In each row, draw a circle around the word that is correctly accented.

1.	noiseless	creaky	doleful
2.	stormy	stopping	shortest
3.	wordless	poorly	adding
4.	preaching	quickly	popping
5.	runner	teller	dweller
6.	childish	impish	devilish
7.	fearful	joyful	wishful
8.	stringy	lucky	kindly
9.	trusting	picking	helping
10.	milky	jerky	foggy

MASTERY REQUIREMENT: 8 correct responses

Indicate mastery on the student response sheet with a check.

FOURTH LEVEL

II. WORD ATTACK SKILLS

A. Structural Analysis

2. Knows accent rules

c. Endings that form syllables are usually unaccented

Name ______________________________

Date ______________________________

Mastery ___________

DIRECTIONS: In each row, draw a circle around the word that is correctly accented.

1.	noise´less	creaky´	doleful´
2.	stormy´	stopping´	short´est
3.	wordless´	poor´ly	adding´
4.	preaching´	quick´ly	popping´
5.	run´ner	teller´	dweller´
6.	childish´	imp´ish	devilish´
7.	fear´ful	joyful´	wishful´
8.	stringy´	luck´y	kindly´
9.	trusting´	pick´ing	helping´
10.	milky´	jerky´	fog´gy

FOURTH LEVEL

II. WORD ATTACK SKILLS A. Structural Analysis 2. Knows accent clues

d. ck followed by a single vowel is accented

OBJECTIVE: The pupil will demonstrate an understanding of the accent rule that ck followed by a single vowel is accented.

DIRECTIONS: Read each of the following words to yourself. Then circle the word in Column A or Column B that is correctly accented.

		Column A	*Column B*
1.	racket	rack et´	(rack´ et)
2.	package	(pack´ age)	pack age´
3.	sickle	(sick´ le)	sick le´
4.	chuckle	chuck le´	(chuck´ le)
5.	shackle	(shack´ le)	shack le´
6.	backer	back er´	(back´ er)
7.	socker	sock er´	(sock´ er)
8.	packer	(pack´ er)	pack er´
9.	sickish	(sick´ ish)	sick ish´
10.	blacken	black en´	(black´ en)

MASTERY REQUIRMENT: 8 correct responses

Indicate mastery on the student response sheet with a check.

FOURTH LEVEL

II. WORD ATTACK SKILLS

A. Structural Analysis

2. Knows accent clues

d. ck followed by a single vowel is accented

Name ______________________

Date ______________________

Mastery __________

DIRECTIONS: Read each of the following words to yourself. Then circle the word in Column A or Column B that is correctly accented.

		Column A	*Column B*
1.	racket	rack et´	rack´ et
2.	package	pack´ age	pack age´
3.	sickle	sick´ le	sick le´
4.	chuckle	chuck le´	chuck´ le
5.	shackle	shack´ le	shack le´
6.	backer	back er´	back´ er
7.	socker	sock er´	sock´ er
8.	packer	pack´ er	pack er´
9.	sickish	sick´ ish	sick ish´
10.	blacken	black en´	black´ en

FOURTH LEVEL

II. WORD ATTACK SKILLS A. Structural Analysis 3. Knows suffixes and prefixes

OBJECTIVE: The pupil will demonstrate a knowledge of prefixes and suffixes.

DIRECTIONS: PART I: Read the word to yourself carefully. Underline the prefix or suffix in the word.

1. moisture
2. connect
3. misplace
4. shortage
5. predict
6. insistence
7. likewise
8. supervision
9. disprove
10. dependent
11. incomplete
12. lofty
13. comfort
14. action
15. triangular
16. pleasant
17. nonskid
18. allowance
19. anticlimax
20. tangling

MASTERY REQUIREMENT: 16 correct responses

Indicate mastery on the student response sheet with a check.

FOURTH LEVEL

II. WORD ATTACK SKILLS

A. Structural Analysis

3. Knows prefixes and suffixes

Name ______________________________

Date ______________________________

Mastery __________

DIRECTIONS: PART I: Read the word to yourself carefully. Underline the prefix or suffix in the word.

1. moisture
2. connect
3. misplace
4. shortage
5. predict
6. insistence
7. likewise
8. supervision
9. disprove
10. dependent
11. incomplete
12. lofty
13. comfort
14. action
15. triangular
16. pleasant
17. nonskid
18. allowance
19. anticlimax
20. tangling

FOURTH LEVEL

II. WORD ATTACK SKILLS A. Structural Analysis 3. Knows suffixes and prefixes

OBJECTIVE: The pupil will demonstrate a knowledge of prefixes and suffixes.

DIRECTIONS: Read each of the words to yourself very carefully. Underline the prefix or suffix in the word.

PART II:

1. deplane
2. postscript
3. absolve
4. melodious
5. indistinct
6. mellowness
7. perfume
8. babyish
9. endure
10. battlement
11. export
12. electric
13. procure
14. humorous
15. interact
16. subway
17. starward
18. expand
19. washable
20. endanger
21. embellish
22. settlement
23. enlist
24. transmit
25. postpone

MASTERY REQUIREMENT: 20 correct responses

Indicate mastery on the student response sheet with a check.

FOURTH LEVEL

II. WORD ATTACK SKILLS

A. Structural Analysis

3. Knows suffixes and prefixes

Name ____________________

Date ____________________

Mastery __________

DIRECTIONS: Read each of the words to yourself very carefully. Underline the prefix or suffix in the word.

PART II:

1. deplane
2. postscript
3. absolve
4. melodious
5. indistinct
6. mellowness
7. perfume
8. babyish
9. endure
10. battlement
11. export
12. electric
13. procure
14. humorous
15. interact
16. subway
17. starward
18 expand
19. washable
20. endanger
21. embellish
22. settlement
23. enlist
24. transmit
25. postpone

FOURTH LEVEL

II. WORD ATTACK SKILLS A. Structural Analysis 3. Knows suffixes and prefixes
a. Suffixes

OBJECTIVE: The pupil will recognize and know the meaning of suffixes.

DIRECTIONS: Read each of the following words and think carefully. Then write the root word, suffix, and the meaning of the suffix on the lines under the correct headings.

NOTE TO TEACHER: Depending on the past learning experiences of the pupil, you may wish to have the pupil write only the root word and the suffix.

PART I:

	ROOT WORD	*SUFFIX*	*MEANING*
1. quickness	quick	ness	being
2. decodable	decode	able	capable of being
3. improvement	improve	ment	result of
4. luscious	lus	cious	abounding in
5. outward	out	ward	in direction of
6. courageous	courage	ous	full of
7. selfish	self	ish	like
8. terrific	terrific	ic	like, made of
9. soundness	sound	ness	being
10. expectant	expect	ant	being
11. mysterious	mystery	ious	abounding in
12. roomette	room	ette	little
13. placement	place	ment	result of
14. booklet	book	let	little
15. dangerous	danger	ous	full of
16. backward	back	ward	in direction of
17. pleasant	please	ant	being
18. honorable	honor	able	capable of being
19. snobbish	snob	ish	like
20. heroic	hero	ic	like, made of

MASTERY REQUIREMENT: 10 correct responses

Indicate mastery on the student response sheet with a check.

FOURTH LEVEL

II. WORD ATTACK SKILLS **Name**________________________

A. Structural Analysis

Date ________________________

3. Knows suffixes and prefixes

a. Suffixes **Mastery** __________

DIRECTIONS:

Option I: Read each of the following words and think carefully. Then write the root word, suffix and the meaning of the suffix on the lines under the correct headings.

Option II: Read the word and think. Write the root word and suffix under the correct headings.

PART I:

	ROOT WORD	*SUFFIX*	*MEANING*
1. quickness	________	______	____________
2. decodable	________	______	____________
3. improvement	________	______	____________
4. luscious	________	______	____________
5. outward	________	______	____________
6. courageous	________	______	____________
7. selfish	________	______	____________
8. terrific	________	______	____________
9. soundness	________	______	____________
10. expectant	________	______	____________
11. mysterious	________	______	____________
12. roomette	________	______	____________
13. placement	________	______	____________
14. booklet	________	______	____________
15. dangerous	________	______	____________
16. backward	________	______	____________
17. pleasant	________	______	____________
18. honorable	________	______	____________
19. snobbish	________	______	____________
20. heroic	________	______	____________

FOURTH LEVEL

II. WORD ATTACK SKILLS A. Structural Analysis 3. Knows suffixes and prefixes

a. Suffixes

OBJECTIVE: The pupil will recognize and know the meaning of suffixes.

DIRECTIONS: PART II

Option 1: Read the word and think. Then write the root word, suffix and the meaning of the suffix on the lines under the correct headings.

Option 2: Read the words carefully. Then write the root word and the suffix on the lines under the correct headings.

	ROOT WORD	*SUFFIX*	*MEANING*
1. different	differ	ent	one who
2. seedling	seed	ling	little
3. attendance	attend	ance	state of being
4. failure	fail	ure	denoting action
5. confidence	confid	ence	state or quality
6. invention	invent	ion	condition or quality
7. acreage	acre	age	collection of
8. vacation	vacat	ion	quality
9. prominence	promin	ence	state or quality
10. mixture	mix	ture	denoting action
11. performance	perform	ance	state of being
12. nestling	nest	ling	little
13. crosswire	cross	wise	ways
14. yardage	yard	age	collection of
15. novelty	novel	ty	state
16. sidewise	side	wise	ways
17. promotion	promot	ion	state or quality
18. excellent	excel	ent	one who
19. unity	uni	ty	state
20. nowise	no	wise	ways

MASTERY REQUIREMENT: 16 correct responses

Indicate mastery on the student response sheet with a check.

FOURTH LEVEL

II. WORD ATTACK SKILLS

Name ______________________

A. Structural Analysis

Date ______________________

3. Knows suffixes and prefixes

a. Suffixes

Mastery __________

DIRECTIONS: PART II

Option 1: Read the word and think. Then write the root word, suffix and the meaning of the suffix on the lines under the correct headings.

Option 2: Read the words carefully. Then write the root word and the suffix on the lines under the correct headings.

	ROOT WORD	*SUFFIX*	*MEANING*
1. different	________	______	______________
2. seedling	________	______	______________
3. attendance	________	______	______________
4. failure	________	______	______________
5. confidence	________	______	______________
6. invention	________	______	______________
7. acreage	________	______	______________
8. vacation	________	______	______________
9. prominence	________	______	______________
10. mixture	________	______	______________
11. performance	________	______	______________
12. nestling	________	______	______________
13. crosswire	________	______	______________
14. yardage	________	______	______________
15. novelty	________	______	______________
16. sidewise	________	______	______________
17. promotion	________	______	______________
18. excellent	________	______	______________
19. unity	________	______	______________
20. nowise	________	______	______________

FOURTH LEVEL

II. WORD ATTACK SKILLS A. Structural Analysis 3. Knows suffixes and prefixes
b. Prefixes

OBJECTIVE: The pupil will demonstrate the ability to recognize prefixes.

DIRECTIONS: PART I

Option 1: Write the prefix, root word and the meaning of the prefix on the line under the correct heading.

Option 2: Write the prefix and root word on the line under the correct heading.

	PREFIX	*ROOT WORD*	*MEANING*
1. mistake	mis	take	wrong
2. disappear	dis	appear	not
3. nonpareil	non	pareil	not
4. invisible	in	visible	not
5. compress	com	press	with
6. misspell	mis	spell	wrong
7. concentrate	con	centrate	with
8. displease	dis	please	not
9. prefix	pre	fix	before
10. antifreeze	anti	freeze	against
11. supersonic	super	sonic	over
12. incorrect	in	correct	not
13. concern	con	cern	with
14. nonfat	non	fat	not
15. antisocial	anti	social	against
16. combine	com	bine	with
17. triangle	tri	angle	three
18. preplan	pre	plan	before
19. triad	tri	ad	three
20. supertax	super	tax	over

MASTERY REQUIREMENT: 16 correct responses

Indicate mastery on the student response sheet with a check.

FOURTH LEVEL

II. WORD ATTACK SKILLS

Name ______________________________

A. Structural Analysis

Date ______________________________

3. Knows suffixes and prefixes

b. Prefixes

Mastery ___________

DIRECTIONS: PART I

Option 1: Write the prefix, root word and the meaning of the prefix on the line under the correct heading.

Option 2: Write the prefix and root word on the line under the correct heading.

	PREFIX	*ROOT WORD*	*MEANING*
1. mistake	_________	____________	________________________
2. disappear	_________	____________	________________________
3. nonpareil	_________	____________	________________________
4. invisible	_________	____________	________________________
5. compress	_________	____________	________________________
6. misspell	_________	____________	________________________
7. concentrate	_________	____________	________________________
8. displease	_________	____________	________________________
9. prefix	_________	____________	________________________
10. antifreeze	_________	____________	________________________
11. supersonic	_________	____________	________________________
12. incorrect	_________	____________	________________________
13. concern	_________	____________	________________________
14. nonfat	_________	____________	________________________
15. antisocial	_________	____________	________________________
16. combine	_________	____________	________________________
17. triangle	_________	____________	________________________
18. preplan	_________	____________	________________________
19. triad	_________	____________	________________________
20. supertax	_________	____________	________________________

FOURTH LEVEL

II. WORD ATTACK SKILLS A. Structural Analysis 3. Knows suffixes and prefixes

b. Prefixes

OBJECTIVE: The pupil will demonstrate knowledge of prefixes.

DIRECTIONS: PART II:

Option 1: Write the prefix, root word and the meaning of the prefix on the line under the correct heading.

Option 2: Write the prefix and root word on the line under the correct heading.

	PREFIX	*ROOT WORD*	*MEANING*
1. submarine	sub	marine	under
2. transverse	trans	verse	across
3. post-mortem	post	mortem	after
4. detain	de	tain	from
5. abstain	ab	stain	from
6. postpone	post	pone	later, after
7. expand	ex	pand	out of
8. embargo	em	bargo	in
9. encase	en	case	in
10. transport	trans	port	across
11. proceed	pro	ceed	before, in front of
12. submerge	sub	merge	under
13. expel	ex	pel	out
14. embattled	em	battled	in
15. interbreed	inter	breed	between
16. obstruct	ob	struct	against
17. encircle	en	circle	in
18. expect	ex	pect	out
19. perform	per	form	do
20. detach	de	tach	from

MASTERY REQUIREMENT: 16 correct responses

Indicate mastery on the student response sheet with a check.

FOURTH LEVEL

II. WORD ATTACK SKILLS **Name** ______________________

A. Structural Analysis

Date ______________________

3. Knows suffixes and prefixes

b. Prefixes **Mastery** __________

DIRECTIONS: PART II:

Option 1: Write the prefix, root word and the meaning of the prefix on the line under the correct heading.

Option 2: Write the prefix and root word on the line under the correct heading.

	PREFIX	*ROOT WORD*	*MEANING*
1. submarine	________	________	________
2. transverse	________	________	________
3. post-mortem	________	________	________
4. detain	________	________	________
5. abstain	________	________	________
6. postpone	________	________	________
7. expand	________	________	________
8. embargo	________	________	________
9. encase	________	________	________
10. transport	________	________	________
11. proceed	________	________	________
12. submerge	________	________	________
13. expel	________	________	________
14. embattled	________	________	________
15. interbreed	________	________	________
16. obstruct	________	________	________
17. encircle	________	________	________
18. expect	________	________	________
19. perform	________	________	________
20. detach	________	________	________

FOURTH LEVEL

II. WORD ATTACK SKILLS B. Phonic Analysis 1. Knows phonic skills

a. Single consonants and blends

OBJECTIVE: The pupil will demonstrate knowledge of the single consonants and blends.

DIRECTIONS—PART I: Look at the pictures carefully. To yourself, say the word each picture represents and draw a line from the picture to the beginning consonant of the word.

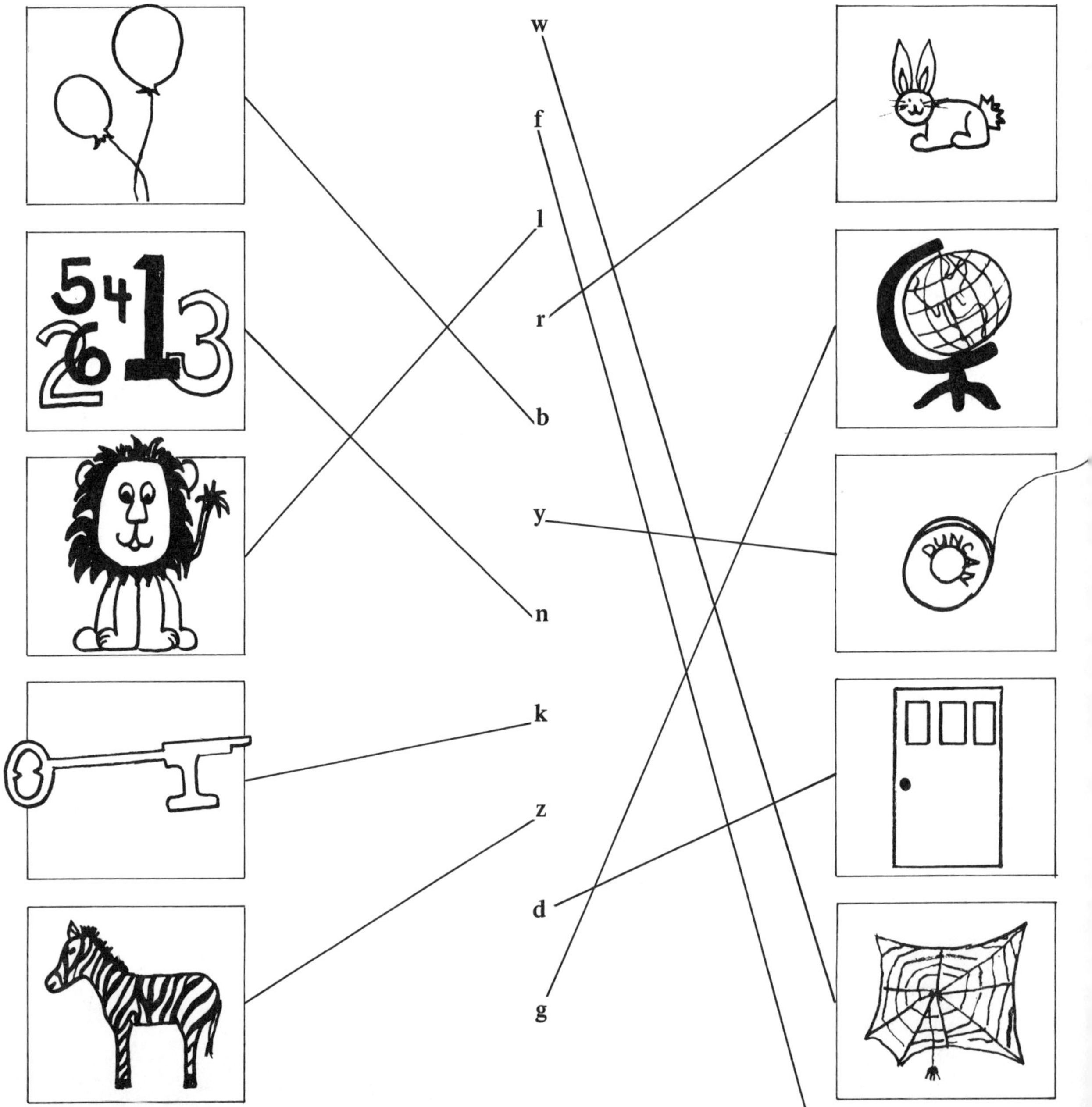

MASTERY REQUIREMENT: All correct

Indicate mastery on the student response sheet with a check.

Only indicate mastery on the skills check list after the pupil has completed all four parts.

FOURTH LEVEL

II. WORD ATTACK SKILLS

Name ______________________________

B. Phonic Analysis

Date ______________________________

1. Knows phonic skills

a. Single consonants and blends

Mastery Part I ____________

DIRECTIONS–PART I: Look at the pictures carefully. To yourself, say the word each picture represents and draw a line from the picture to the beginning consonant of the word.

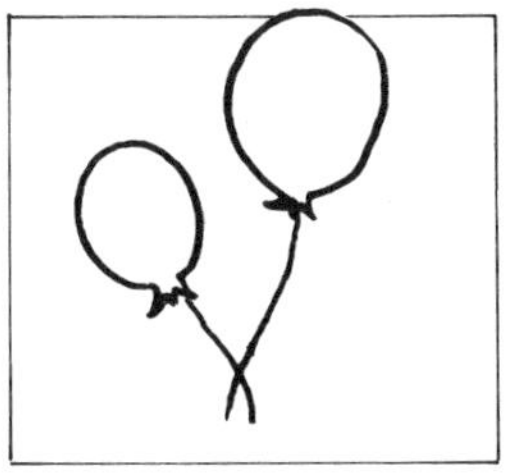

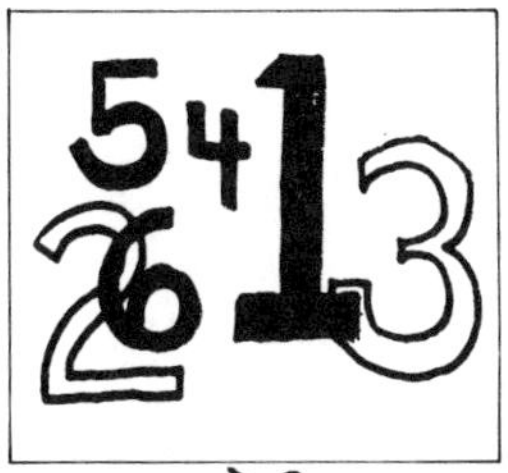

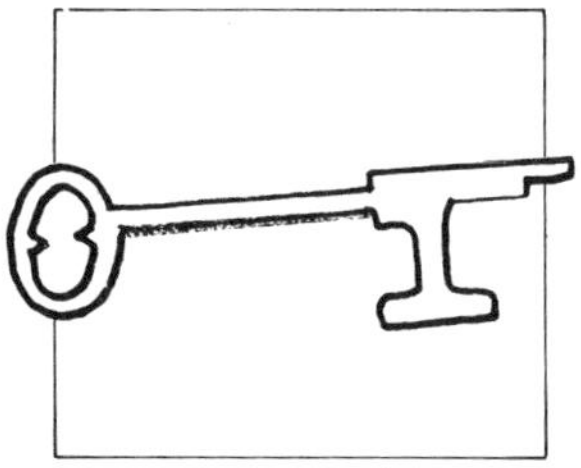

w

f

l

r

b

y

n

k

z

d

g

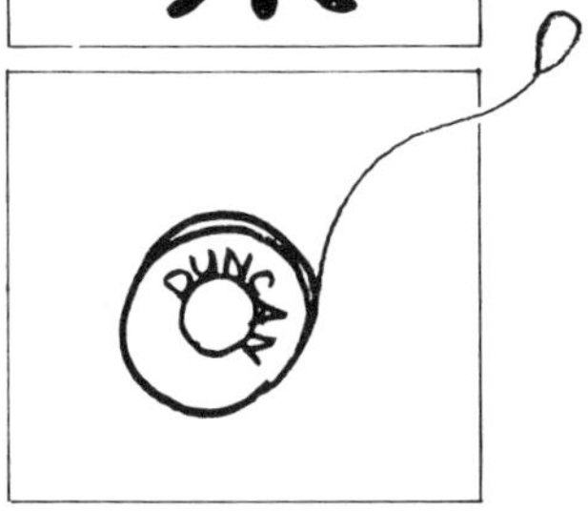

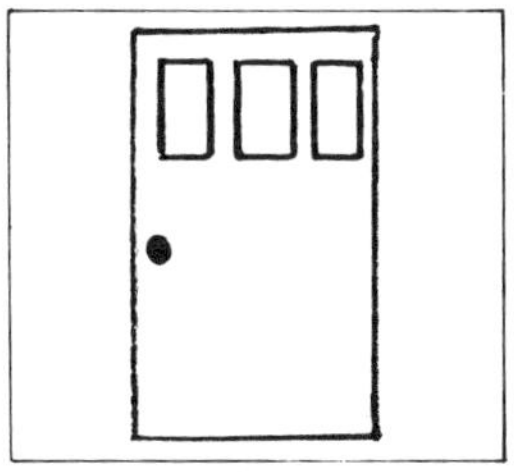

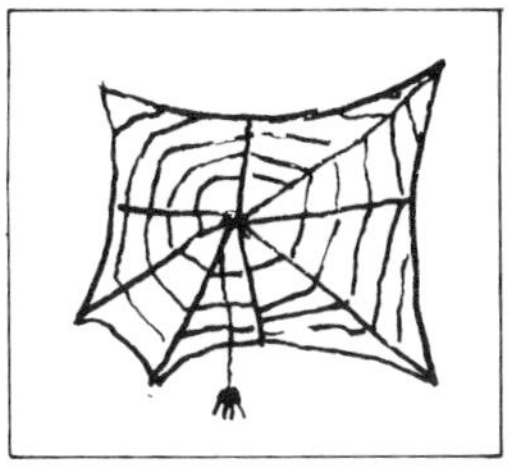

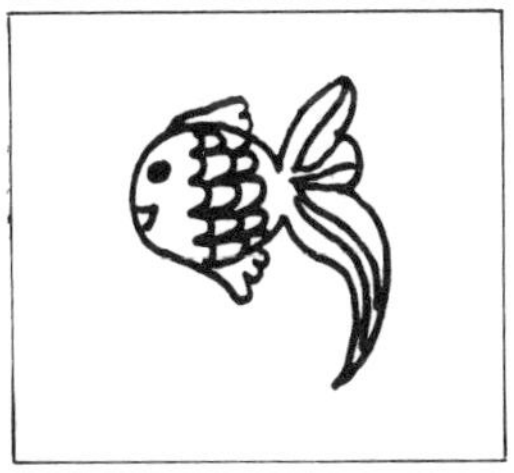

FOURTH LEVEL

II. WORD ATTACK SKILLS B. Phonic Analysis 1. Knows phonic skills

a. Single consonants and blends

DIRECTIONS–PART II: Look at the pictures carefully. To yourself say the word each picture represents and draw a line from the picture to the beginning consonant of the word.

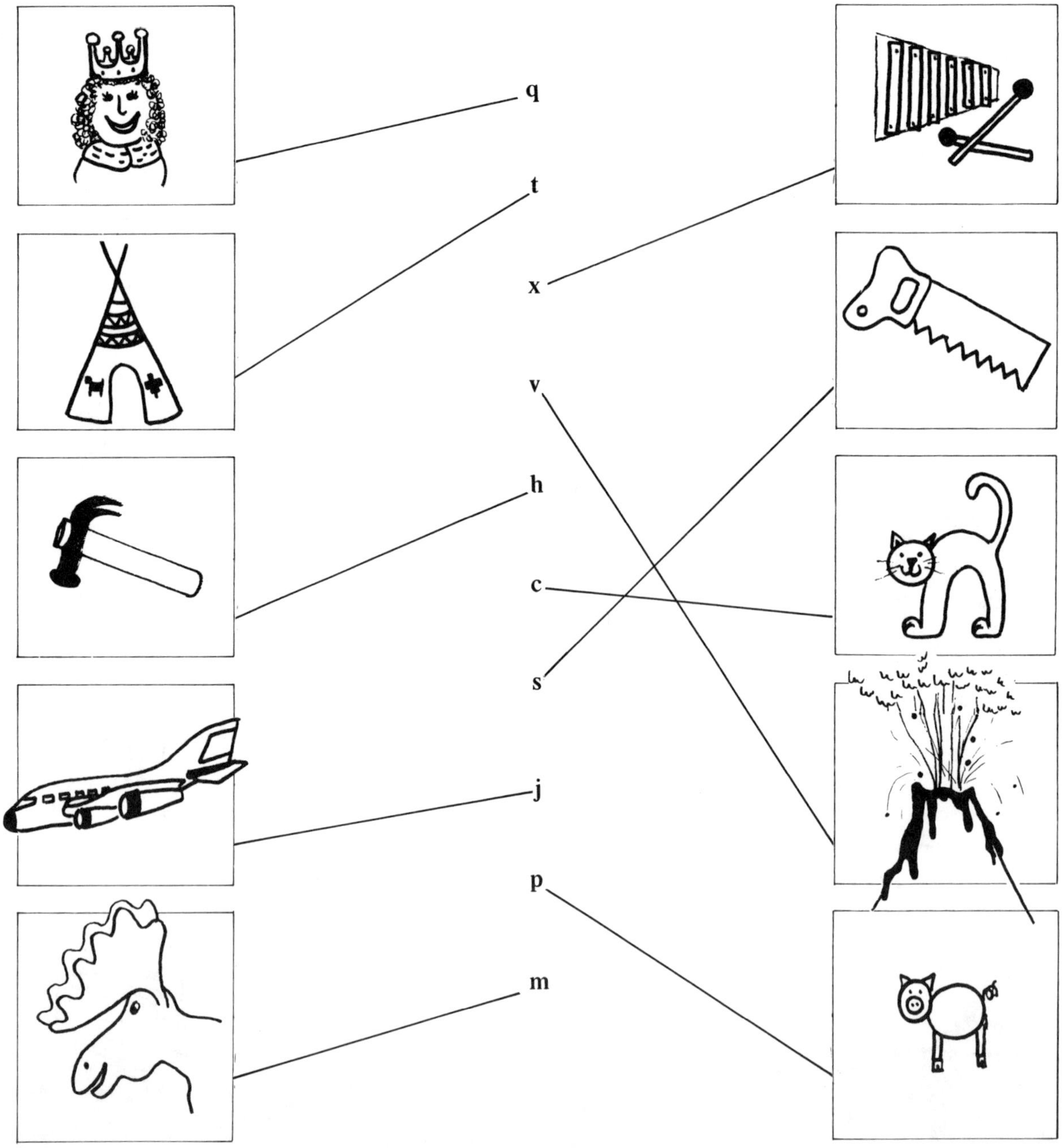

MASTERY REQUIREMENT: All correct

Indicate mastery on the student response sheet with a check.

Only indicate mastery on the skills check list after the pupil has completed all four parts.

FOURTH LEVEL

II. WORD ATTACK SKILLS

B. Phonic Analysis

1. Knows phonic skills

a. Single consonants and blends

Name ______________________________

Date ______________________________

Mastery Part II ___________

DIRECTIONS–PART II: Look at the pictures carefully. To yourself say the word each picture represents and draw a line from the picture to the beginning consonant of the word.

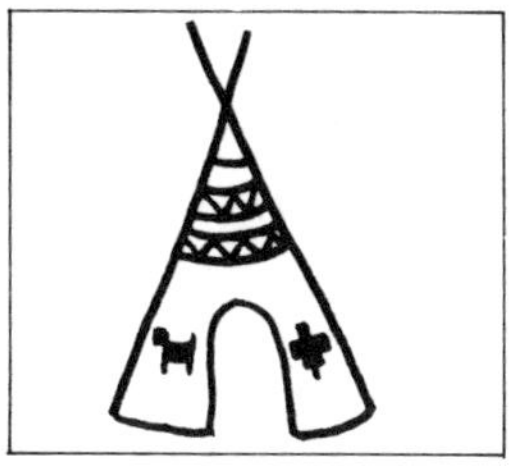

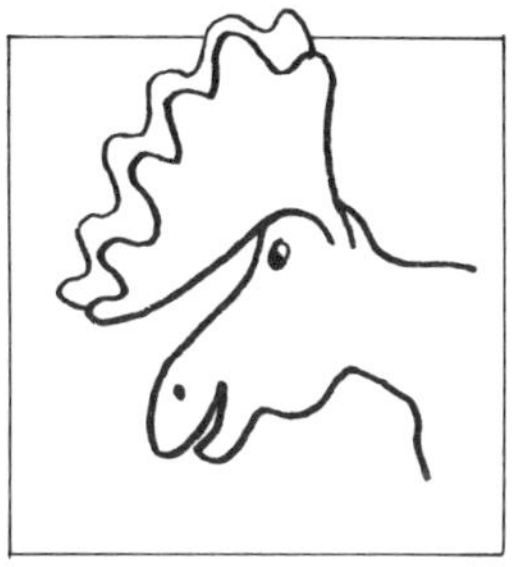

q

t

x

v

h

c

s

j

p

m

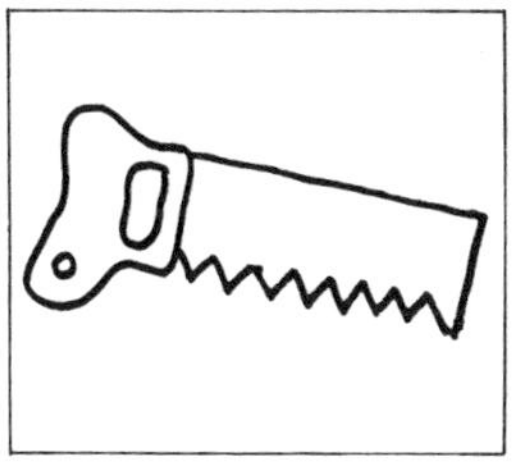

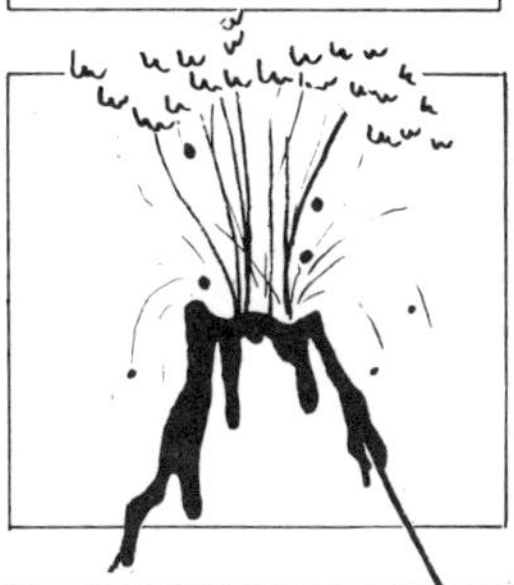

FOURTH LEVEL

II. WORD ATTACK SKILLS B. Phonic Analysis 1. Knows phonic skills

a. Single consonants and blends

DIRECTIONS–PART III: Look at the pictures carefully. To yourself, say the word each picture represents and draw a line from the picture to the beginning consonant blend of the word.

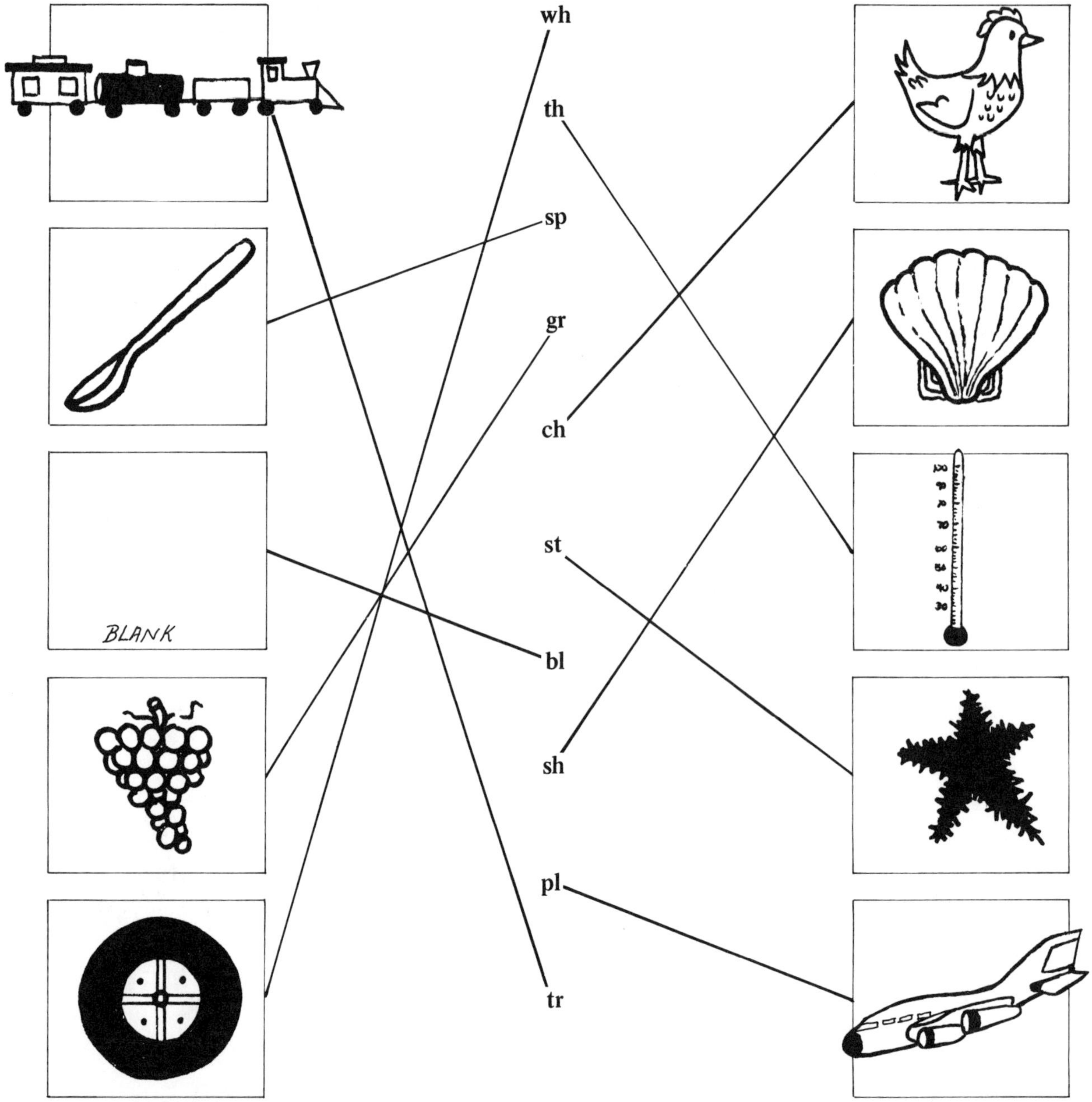

MASTERY REQUIREMENT: All correct

Indicate mastery on the student response sheet with a check.

Only indicate mastery on the skills check list after the pupil has completed all four parts.

FOURTH LEVEL

II. WORD ATTACK SKILLS

B. Phonic Analysis

1. Knows phonic skills

a. Single consonants and blends

Name ______________________________

Date ______________________________

Mastery Part III ___________

DIRECTIONS—PART III: Look at the pictures carefully. To yourself, say the word each picture represents and draw a line from the picture to the beginning consonant blend of the word.

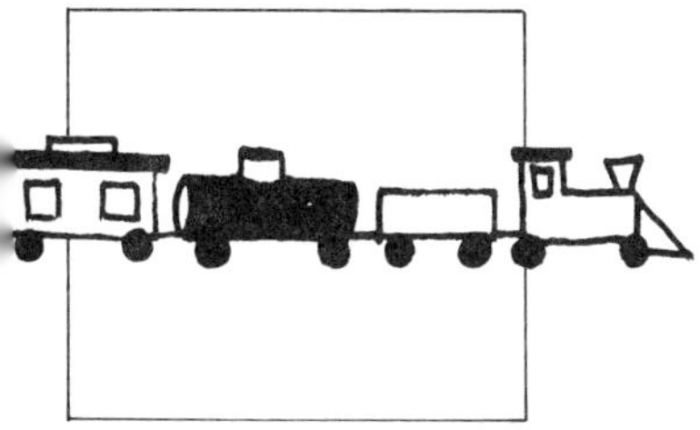

wh

th

sp

gr

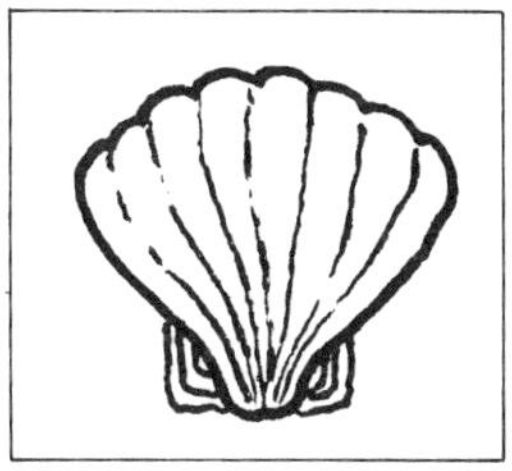

ch

st

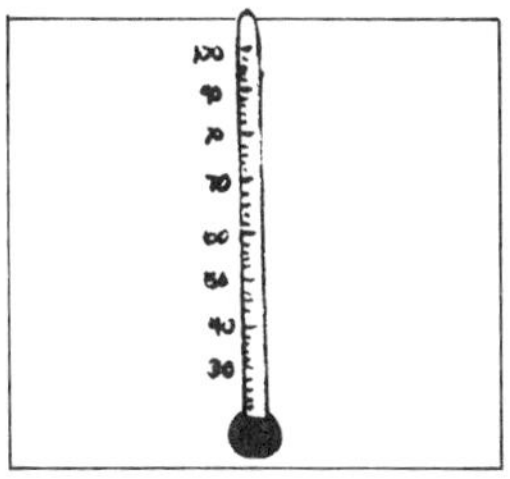

bl

sh

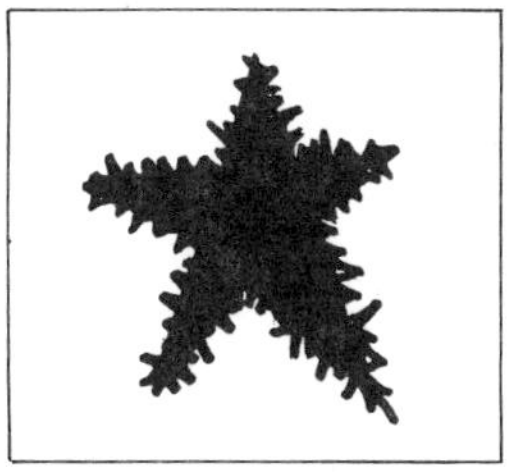

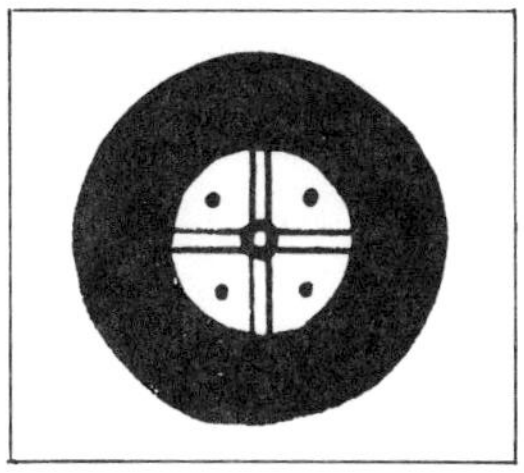

pl

tr

FOURTH LEVEL

II. WORD ATTACK SKILLS B. Phonic Analysis 1. **Knows phonic skills**

a. **Single consonants and blends**

DIRECTIONS–PART IV: Look at the pictures carefully. To yourself, say the word each picture represents and draw a line from the picture to the beginning consonant blend of the word.

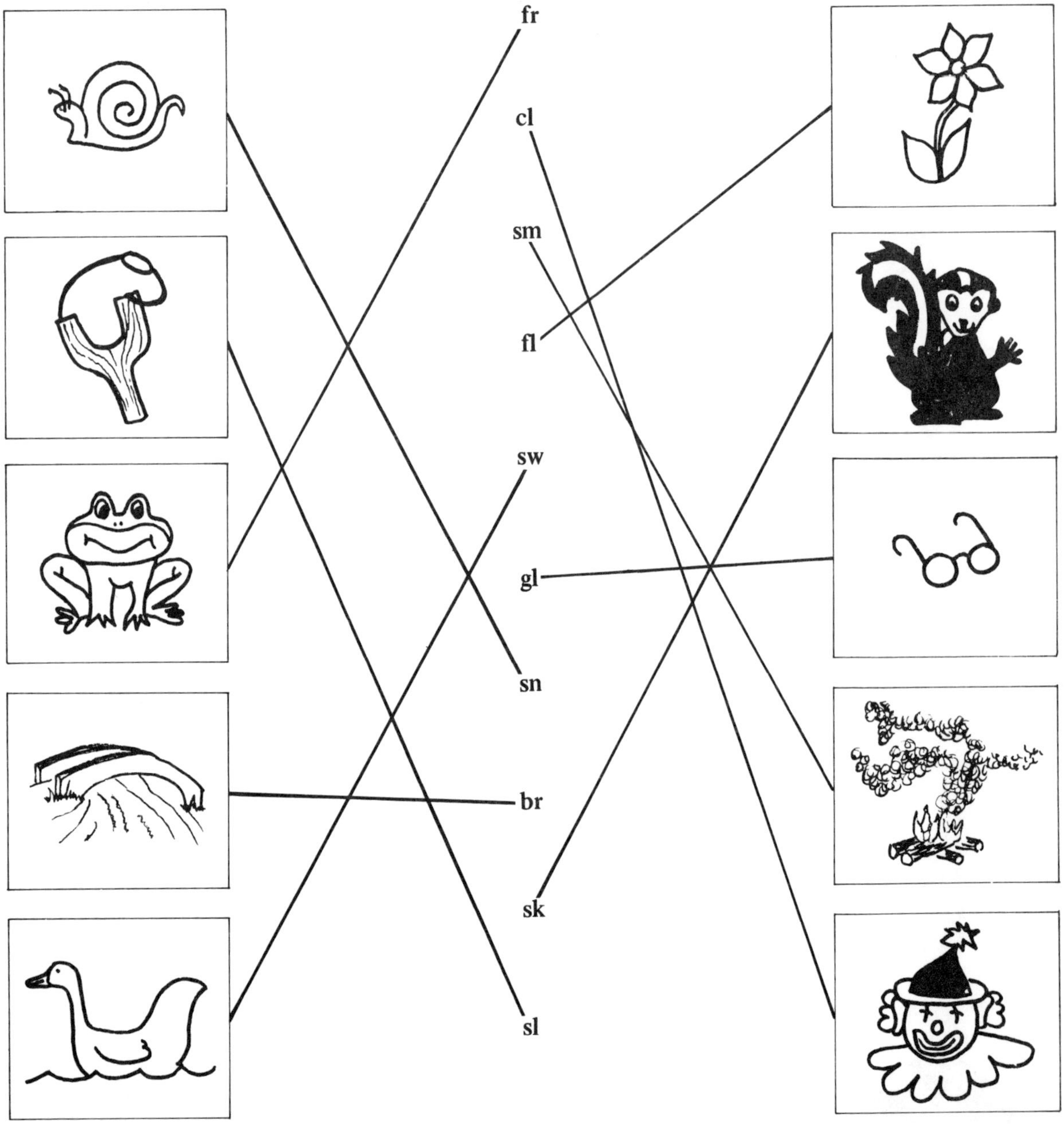

MASTERY REQUIREMENT: All correct

Indicate mastery on the student response sheet wih a check.

The pupil has now completed the four parts of this objective, indicate mastery on the skills check

FOURTH LEVEL

II. WORD ATTACK SKILLS

B. Phonic Analysis

1. Knows phonic skills

a. Single consonants and blends

Name ______________________

Date ______________________

Mastery Part IV __________

DIRECTIONS–PART IV: Look at the pictures carefully. To yourself, say the word each picture represents and draw a line from the picture to the beginning consonant blend of the word.

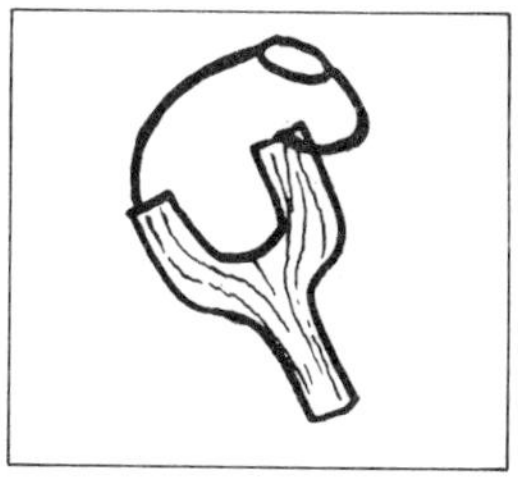

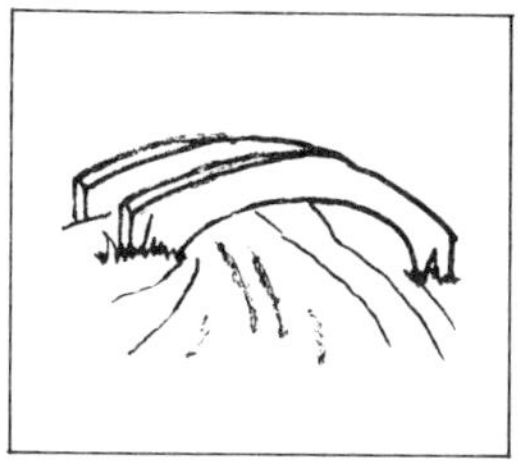

fr

cl

sm

fl

sw

gl

sn

br

sk

sl

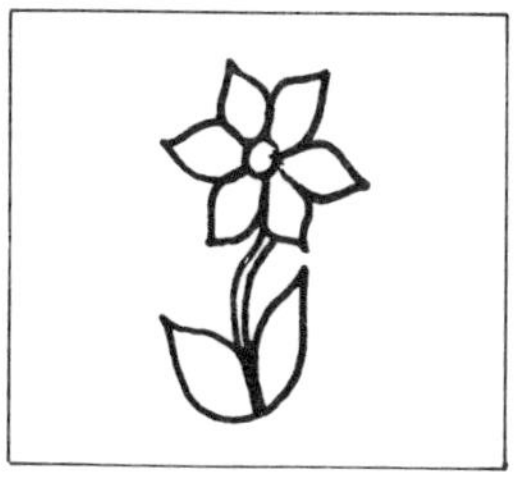

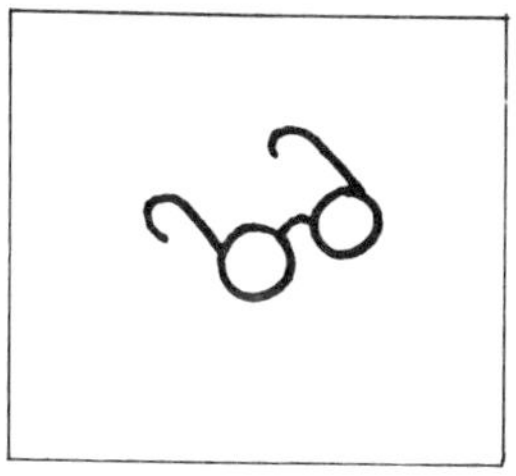

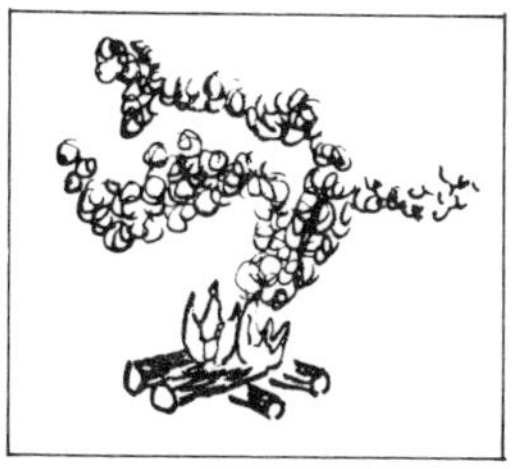

FOURTH LEVEL

II. WORD ATTACK SKILLS B. Phonic Analysis 1. Knows phonic skills

b. Short and long vowels

OBJECTIVE: The pupil will demonstrate a knowledge of long and short vowels.

DIRECTIONS: Read the list of words carefully. Then place a breve (∪) over the short vowel sound, a macron (¯) over the long vowel sound and a slash (/) through the silent vowel.

1. ădd	11. ŏdd
2. fĭfth	12. rŭst
3. bĕt	13. sēa̸
4. clăm	14. boil
5. shŭt	15. cōcō
6. drīve̸	16. bŭzz
7. stŭff	17. sĭlk
8. cōde̸	18. gāte̸
9. cŏb	19. dēa̸l
10. slĕd	20. līfe̸

MASTERY REQUIREMENT: 16 correct responses

Indicate mastery on the student response sheet with a check.

FOURTH LEVEL

II. WORD ATTACK SKILLS

B. Phonic Analysis

1. Knows phonic skills

b. Short and long vowels

Name ____________________

Date ____________________

Mastery __________

DIRECTIONS: Read the list of words carefully. Then place a breve (◡) over the short vowel sound, a macron (—) over the long vowel sound and a slash (/) through the silent vowel.

1. add
2. fifth
3. bet
4. clam
5. shut
6. drive
7. stuff
8. code
9. cob
10. sled
11. odd
12. rust
13. sea
14. boil
15. coco
16. buzz
17. silk
18. gate
19. deal
20. life

FOURTH LEVEL

II. WORD ATTACK SKILLS B. Phonic Analysis 1. Knows phonic skills

c. Vowel teams

OBJECTIVE: The pupil will demonstrate an understanding of the vowel teams by pronouncing correctly words made up of vowel teams.

DIRECTIONS: Have the pupil read the list of words to you to verify the pronunciation and the pupil's ability to recognize the vowel teams. Record on the pupil's response sheet the words pronounced correctly.

1. sleep	16. sea
2. main	17. sway
3. lay	18. cause
4. automobile	19. reason
5. saw	20. broad
6. coat	21. awful
7. hook	22. oil
8. weed	23. meek
9. noise	24. clay
10. wound	25. paid
11. stay	26. shook
12. realize	27. towel
13. know	28. soy
14. royal	29. would
15. claim	30. taught

MASTERY REQUIREMENT: 25 correct pronounced

Indicate mastery on the student response sheet with a check.

FOURTH LEVEL

II. WORD ATTACK SKILLS

B. Phonic Analysis

1. Knows phonic skills

c. Vowel teams

Name ____________________

Date ____________________

Mastery ________

DIRECTIONS: Read this list of words to your teacher.

____	1.	sleep	____	16.	sea
____	2.	main	____	17.	sway
____	3.	lay	____	18.	cause
____	4.	automobile	____	19.	reason
____	5.	saw	____	20.	broad
____	6.	coat	____	21.	awful
____	7.	hook	____	22.	oil
____	8.	weed	____	23.	meek
____	9.	noise	____	24.	clay
____	10.	wound	____	25.	paid
____	11.	stay	____	26.	shook
____	12.	realize	____	27.	towel
____	13.	know	____	28.	soy
____	14.	royal	____	29.	would
____	15.	claim	____	30.	taught

FOURTH LEVEL

II. WORD ATTACK SKILLS B. Phonic Analysis 2. Knows vowel rules

OBJECTIVE: The pupil will demonstrate knowledge of the four vowel rules at the fourth level.

DIRECTIONS: Read the following words carefully. Mark the vowel with a macron (—) if the vowel is long, a breve (◡) if the vowel is short, and a slash (/) if the vowel is silent.

1. sāy̸
2. gāze̸
3. ănȳ
4. Bĭllȳ
5. spēa̸k
6. pēa̸s
7. ā
8. Bĕckȳ
9. spōke̸
10. hī
11. brĭghtlȳ
12. rīde̸
13. Ălĭ
14. sēe̸k
15. ŭnĭt
16. ūse̸

MASTERY REQUIREMENT: 12 correct responses

Indicate mastery on the student response sheet with a check.

FOURTH LEVEL

II. WORD ATTACK SKILLS

B. Phonic Analysis

2. Knows vowel rules

Name ______________________________

Date ______________________________

Mastery ___________

DIRECTIONS: Read the following words carefully. Mark the vowel with a macron (—) if the vowel is long, a breve (◡) if the vowel is short, and a slash (/) if the vowel is silent.

1. say
2. gaze
3. any
4. Billy
5. speak
6. peas
7. a
8. Becky
9. spoke
10. hi
11. brightly
12. ride
13. Ali
14. seek
15. unit
16. use

FOURTH LEVEL

II. WORD ATTACK SKILLS B. Phonic Analysis 2. Knows vowel rules

a. In attacking a vowel sound try first the short sound; if the word then doesn't make sense try the long sound

OBJECTIVE: The pupil will demonstrate knowledge of the word attack skill that in attacking a vowel sound, the short sound is tried first and if the word doesn't make sense, then the long sound is tried.

DIRECTIONS: Have the pupil read the list of words. Notice how the pupil attacks the words. Pay specific attention to see if the word attack rule stated above is observed. On the pupil's response sheet, indicate those words which are pronounced correctly.

1. champion	11. gaping
2. collector	12. funeral
3. restaurant	13. chagrin
4. scrapbook	14. jovial
5. percussion	15. genial
6. racket	16. jaguar
7. silver	17. incense
8. musky	18. midge
9. fungus	19. creased
10. waddle	20. picture

MASTERY REQUIREMENT: 16 correct responses

Indicate mastery on the student response sheet with a check.

FOURTH LEVEL

II. WORD ATTACK SKILLS

B. Phonic Analysis

2. Knows vowel rules

a. In attacking a vowel sound try first the short sound; if the word then doesn't make sense try the long sound

Name ______________________

Date ______________________

Mastery __________

DIRECTIONS: Read this list of words to your teacher.

____	1.	champion	____	11.	gaping
____	2.	collector	____	12.	funeral
____	3.	restaurant	____	13.	chagrin
____	4.	scrapbook	____	14.	jovial
____	5.	percussion	____	15.	genial
____	6.	racket	____	16.	jaguar
____	7.	silver	____	17.	incense
____	8.	musky	____	18.	midge
____	9.	fungus	____	19.	creased
____	10.	waddle	____	20.	picture

FOURTH LEVEL

II. WORD ATTACK SKILLS B. Phonic Analysis 2. Knows vowel rules

b. Vowels are usually short when they appear as single vowels and are followed by a consonant

OBJECTIVE: The pupil will demonstrate knowledge of the word attack skill that vowels are usually short when they appear as single vowels and are followed by a consonant.

DIRECTIONS: Read each of the following words. Study the way the word is divided into syllables and then mark the first vowel with a macron (¯) if the vowel is long or a breve (˘) if the vowel is short.

1.	abroad	ă broad
2.	abundant	ă bun dant
3.	elk	ĕlk
4.	eleven	ĕ lev en
5.	eject	ĕ ject
6.	equip	ĕ quip
7.	above	ă bove
8.	erode	ĕ rode
9.	echo	ĕ cho
10.	abandon	ă ban don

MASTERY REQUIREMENT: 8 correct responses

Indicate mastery on the student response sheet with a check.

FOURTH LEVEL

II. WORD ATTACK SKILLS

B. Phonic Analysis

2. Knows vowel rules

b. Vowels are usually short when they appear as single vowels and are followed by a consonant

Name ____________________

Date ____________________

Mastery __________

DIRECTIONS: Read each of the following words. Study the way the word is divided into syllables and then mark the first vowel with a macron (—) if the vowel is long or a breve (∪) if the vowel is short.

1.	abroad	a broad
2.	abundant	a bun dant
3.	elk	elk
4.	eleven	e lev en
5.	eject	e ject
6.	equip	e quip
7.	above	a bove
8.	erode	e rode
9.	echo	e cho
10.	abandon	a ban don

FOURTH LEVEL

II. WORD ATTACK SKILLS B. Phonic Analysis 2. Knows vowel rules

c. Vowels are usually given the long sound when they appcar alone and are the last letters of a word

OBJECTIVE: The pupil will demonstrate an understanding of the vowel rule that vowels are usually given the long sound when they appear alone and are the last letters of a word.

DIRECTIONS: Read the following words carefully. Then mark the last vowel sound by placing a breve (◡) if the vowel sound is short and a macron (¯) if the vowel sound is long.

1. greedy	greed ȳ
2. studio	stu diō
3. echo	ech ō
4. slippery	slip per ȳ
5. slavery	sla ver ȳ
6. murky	murk ȳ
7. hosiery	ho sier ȳ
8. lusty	lust ȳ
9. crafty	craft ȳ
10. nunnery	nun ner ȳ

MASTERY REQUIREMENT: 8 correct responses

Indicate mastery on the student response sheet with a check.

FOURTH LEVEL

II. WORD ATTACK SKILLS

Name ____________________

B. Phonic Analysis

Date ____________________

2. Knows vowel rules

c. Vowels are usually given the long sound when they appear alone and are the last letters of a word

Mastery __________

DIRECTIONS: Read the following words carefully. Then mark the last vowel sound by placing a breve (˘) if the vowel sound is short and a macron (¯) if the vowel sound is long.

1.	greedy	greed y
2.	studio	stu dio
3.	echo	ech o
4.	slippery	slip per y
5.	slavery	sla ver y
6.	murky	murk y
7.	hosiery	ho sier y
8.	lusty	lust y
9.	crafty	craft y
10.	nunnery	nun ner y

FOURTH LEVEL

II. WORD ATTACK SKILLS B. Phonic Analysis 2. Knows vowel rules

d. When two vowels appear together in a word, the first vowel is long and the second is silent

OBJECTIVE: The pupil will demonstrate an understanding of the vowel rule that when two vowels appear together in a word the first vowel is long and the second is silent.

DIRECTIONS: Read the list of words carefully. Then place a breve (˘) over the short vowel sound, a macron (¯) over the long vowel sound, and a slash (/) through the silent letter of the first syllable of these words.

1. hāi̸l
2. bēa̸m
3. pēa̸k
4. prāi̸se
5. clāi̸m
6. bāi̸t
7. whēe̸ze
8. sēi̸ze
9. dȳe̸
10. knēa̸d

MASTERY REQUIREMENT: 8 correct responses

Indicate mastery on the student response sheet with a check.

FOURTH LEVEL

II. WORD ATTACK SKILLS

Name ______________________________

B. Phonic Analysis

Date ______________________________

2. Knows vowel rules

d. When two vowels appear together in a word the first vowel is long and the second is silent

Mastery __________

DIRECTIONS: Read the list of words carefully. Then place a breve (˘) over the short vowel sound, a macron (¯) over the long vowel sound, and a slash (/) through the silent letter of the first syllable of these words.

1. hail
2. beam
3. peak
4. praise
5. claim
6. bait
7. wheeze
8. seize
9. dye
10. knead

FOURTH LEVEL

II. WORD ATTACK SKILLS B. Phonic Analysis 2. Knows vowel rules

e. **In short words containing two vowels where one of the vowels is a final c, the first vowel will have a long sound while the final e is silent**

OBJECTIVE: The pupil will demonstrate knowledge of the vowel rule that in a short word containing two vowels where one of the vowels is a final e, the first vowel will have a long sound while the final e is silent.

DIRECTIONS: Read the following words carefully. Re-write the word on the line beside the word, placing a breve (˘) over the vowels with the short vowel sound, a macron (¯) over the vowels with a long vowel sound, and a slash (/) through the vowel if the vowel is silent.

1. glide glīde̸
2. cope cōpe̸
3. ache āche̸
4. lope lōpe̸
5. male māle̸
6. flute flūte̸
7. scale scāle̸
8. rage rāge̸
9. mane māne̸
10. cone cōne̸

MASTERY REQUIREMENT: 8 correct responses

Indicate mastery on the student response sheet with a check.

FOURTH LEVEL

II. WORD ATTACK SKILLS

Name ______________________

B. Phonic Analysis

Date ______________________

2. Knows vowel rules

e. In short words containing two vowels where one of the vowels is a final e, the first vowel will have a long sound while the final e is silent

Mastery __________

DIRECTIONS: Read the following words carefully. Re-write the word on the line beside the word, placing a breve (◡) over the vowels with the short vowel sound, a macron (¯) over the vowels with a long vowel sound, and a slash (/) through the vowel if the vowel is silent.

1. glide ______________

2. cope ______________

3. ache ______________

4. lope ______________

5. male ______________

6. flute ______________

7. scale ______________

8. rage ______________

9. mane ______________

10. cone ______________

FOURTH LEVEL

II. WORD ATTACK SKILLS **C. Uses Dictionary and Glossary** **1. Alphabetical order** **a. Order of letters in alphabet**

OBJECTIVE: The pupil will demonstrate a knowledge of the order of letters in the alphabet.

DIRECTIONS: Look at the grouping of letters by each number. Put these letters in the correct order on the blank line.

1.	a q l o	a l o q
2.	d j z s	d j s z
3.	u h i c	c h i u
4.	f t m i	f i m t
5.	y e s l	e l s y
6.	k t d w	d k t w
7.	i a w e	a e i w
8.	r s o k	k o r s
9.	u m g l	g l m u
10.	e v s t	e s t v
11.	n u d r	d n r u
12.	o c u z	c o u z
13.	r e w j	e j r w
14.	g b x e	b e g x
15.	z p g v	g p v z
16.	b k e f	b e f k

MASTERY REQUIREMENT: 14 correct responses

Indicate mastery on the student response sheet with a check.

FOURTH LEVEL

II. WORD ATTACK SKILLS

C. Uses Dictionary and Glossary

1. Alphabetical order

a. Order of letters in alphabet

Name ______________________

Date ______________________

Mastery __________

DIRECTIONS: Look at the grouping of letters by each number. Put these letters in the correct order on the blank line.

1. a q l o ______________________
2. d j z s ______________________
3. u h i c ______________________
4. f t m i ______________________
5. y e s l ______________________
6. k t d w ______________________
7. i a w e ______________________
8. r s o k ______________________
9. u m g l ______________________
10. e v s t ______________________
11. n u d r ______________________
12. o c u z ______________________
13. r e w j ______________________
14. g b x e ______________________
15. z p g v ______________________
16. b k e f ______________________

FOURTH LEVEL

II. WORD ATTACK SKILLS **C. Uses Dictionary and Glossary** **1. Alphabetical order**

b. Alphabetical arrangement of words

OBJECTIVE: The pupil will demonstrate the ability to put words in alphabetical order.

DIRECTIONS: Study the list of words carefully. Now, write the words in alphabetical order.

rooster	wire	a	allowance	n	native
X-ray	olive	b	broadcast	o	olive
index	cracker	c	cracker	p	pigeon
allowance	museum	d	danger	q	quiver
seventeen	garbage	e	evening	r	rooster
native	upset	f	feast	s	seventeen
danger	hollow	g	garbage	t	talent
vehicle	talent	h	hollow	u	upset
feast	young	i	index	v	vehicle
quiver	jazz	j	jazz	w	wire
kangaroo	evening	k	kangaroo	x	X-ray
zebra	lantern	l	lantern	y	young
broadcast	pigeon	m	museum	z	zebra

MASTERY REQUIREMENT: All correct

Indicate mastery on the student response sheet with a check.

FOURTH LEVEL

II. WORD ATTACK SKILLS

Name ____________________

C. Uses Dictionary and Glossary

Date ____________________

1. Alphabetical order

b. Alphabetical arrangement or words

Mastery __________

DIRECTIONS: Study the list of words carefully. Now, write the words in alphabetical order.

rooster	wire	a	____________	n	____________
X-ray	olive	b	____________	o	____________
index	cracker	c	____________	p	____________
allowance	museum	d	____________	q	____________
seventeen	garbage	e	____________	r	____________
native	upset	f	____________	s	____________
danger	hollow	g	____________	t	____________
vehicle	talent	h	____________	u	____________
feast	young	i	____________	v	____________
quiver	jazz	j	____________	w	____________
kangaroo	evening	k	____________	x	____________
zebra	lantern	l	____________	y	____________
broadcast	pigeon	m	____________	z	____________

FOURTH LEVEL

II. WORD ATTACK SKILLS   C. Uses Dictionary and Glossary   2. Knows to divide the dictionary to determine in which 1/3 the word may be found

OBJECTIVE: The pupil will demonstrate the ability to determine which third of the dictionary a word may be found.

DIRECTIONS: Study each word carefully and decide if you would find the word in the beginning (a-h), middle (i-q), or the end (r-z) part of the dictionary. Write beginning, middle, or end on the line next to the word.

Beginning – a-h
Middle – i-q
End – r-z

1.	rhythm	end
2.	chute	beginning
3.	focus	beginning
4.	massive	middle
5.	tension	end
6.	sailors	end
7.	beggar	beginning
8.	jaws	middle
9.	powerful	middle
10.	glorious	beginning
11.	honor	beginning
12.	visit	end
13.	lark	middle
14.	zoo	end
15.	wrench	end
16.	novel	middle
17.	dough	beginning
18.	yoke	end
19.	key	middle
20.	X-ray	end

MASTERY REQUIREMENT: 16 correct responses

Indicate mastery on the student response sheet with a check.

FOURTH LEVEL

II. WORD ATTACK SKILLS

C. Uses Dictionary and Glossary

2. Knows to divide the dictionary to determine in which 1/3 the word may be found

Name ______________________

Date ______________________

Mastery __________

DIRECTIONS: Study each word carefully and decide if you would find the word in the beginning (a-h), middle (i-q), or the end (r-z) part of the dictionary. Write beginning, middle, or end on the line next to the word.

Beginning – a-h
Middle – i-q
End – r-z

1. rhythm ______________________
2. chute ______________________
3. focus ______________________
4. massive ______________________
5. tension ______________________
6. sailors ______________________
7. beggar ______________________
8. jaws ______________________
9. powerful ______________________
10. glorious ______________________
11. honor ______________________
12. visit ______________________
13. lark ______________________
14. zoo ______________________
15. wrench ______________________
16. novel ______________________
17. dough ______________________
18. yoke ______________________
19. key ______________________
20. X-ray ______________________

FOURTH LEVEL

II. WORD ATTACK SKILLS C. Uses Dictionary and Glossary 3. **Knows the meaning and use of the phonetic spelling that follows in parenthesis each word in the dictionary**

OBJECTIVE: The pupil will demonstrate the ability to use the phonetic spelling that follows in parenthesis each word in the dictionary.

DIRECTIONS: Look at the phonetic spelling and on the line write the correct spelling of the word.

1. fās — face
2. dē pō — depot
3. trăns fûr — transfer
4. swĕl — swell
5. rĭlī — rely
6. fŭn əl — funnel
7. hā stĕ — hasty
8. ĕk o — echo
9. ā kər — acre
10. bā — bay

MASTERY REQUIREMENT: 7 correct responses

Indicate mastery on the student response sheet with a check.

FOURTH LEVEL

II. WORD ATTACK SKILLS

Name ______________________

C. Uses Dictionary and Glossary

Date ______________________

3. Knows the meaning and use of the phonetic spelling that follows in parenthesis each word in the dictionary

Mastery __________

DIRECTIONS: Look at the phonetic spelling and on the line write the correct spelling of the word.

1. fās ______________________

2. dē pō ______________________

3. trăns fûr ______________________

4. swĕl ______________________

5. rĭlī ______________________

6. fŭn əl ______________________

7. hā stĕ ______________________

8. ĕk o ______________________

9. ā kər ______________________

10. bā ______________________

FOURTH LEVEL

II. WORD ATTACK SKILLS C. Uses Dictionary and Glossary 4. Knows the use of the pronunciation key

OBJECTIVE: The pupil will demonstrate the ability to use the pronunciation key.

DIRECTIONS: Look up the following words in your dictionary. Write the phonetic spelling and then pronounce the words. If the word is pronounced correctly, place a check on the line to the right of the word.

		Phonetic Spelling	Pronunciation
1.	technician	tek nish´ ən	______
2.	descent	di sĕ̈nt´	______
3.	inoculation	in ok´ y əlā´ shən	______
4.	girdle	ger´ dl	______
5.	argument	ör´ gyə mənt	______
6.	erosion	i rō´ zhən	______
7.	nomadic	nō mad´ ic	______
8.	gaudy	gô´ dē	______
9.	ancestor	ȧn´ ses tər	______
10.	reliable	ri lī´ əbl	______

Dictionaries may vary in the phonetic spelling.

MASTERY REQUIREMENT: 8 correct responses

Indicate mastery on the student response sheet with a check.

FOURTH LEVEL

II. WORD ATTACK SKILLS

C. Uses Dictionary and Glossary

4. Knows the use of the pronunciation key

Name ______________________

Date ______________________

Mastery __________

DIRECTIONS: Look up the following words in your dictionary. Write the phonetic spelling and then pronounce the words to your teacher.

	Phonetic Spelling	Pronunciation
1. technician	______________	______________
2. descent	______________	______________
3. inoculation	______________	______________
4. girdle	______________	______________
5. argument	______________	______________
6. erosion	______________	______________
7. nomadic	______________	______________
8. gaudy	______________	______________
9. ancestor	______________	______________
10. reliable	______________	______________

FOURTH LEVEL

II. WORD ATTACK SKILLS C. Uses Dictionary and Glossary 5. **Knows to select the meaning which fits best according to the context in which the word is used**

OBJECTIVE: The pupil will demonstrate the ability to select the meaning which fits best according to the context in which the word is used.

DIRECTIONS: Read the sentences, paying close attention to the underlined word and the definition below the sentences. Then on the line in front of the number indicate the meaning which fits best according to the context of the sentence.

_b_ 1. The Indians pounded the corn into meal.

_a_ 2. Kathryn prepared a delicious meal for her sisters.

- a. breakfast, lunch, dinner
- b. grain ground up
- c. dry and powdery

_c_ 3. I tire easily.

_a_ 4. Marguerite's bicycle had a flat tire.

- a. ring of rubber that is filled around the rim of a wheel
- b. boring
- c. make weary

_b_ 5. The shot woke me up.

_c_ 6. Greg is a good shot.

- a. breath
- b. sound made by a weapon
- c. person who shoots

_a_ 7. The barge moved slowly up the river.

_b_ 8. Glen will barge through the door any minute now.

- a. flat-bottom boat used for freight
- b. interrupt in a clumsy, rude manner
- c. a crowd

_c_ 9. As Louise spoke, she stroked the cat.

_a_ 10. The stroke of the clock frightened the burglar.

- a. a sound of a striking clock
- b. action
- c. to caress with the hand

_b_ 11. Kathryn is a brave person.

_a_ 12. The braves were on the warpath.

- a. Indian warrior
- b. having courage
- c. shorstop

MASTERY REQUIREMENT: 10 correct responses

Indicate mastery on the student response sheet with a check.

FOURTH LEVEL

II. WORD ATTACK SKILLS

Name ______________________

C. Uses Dictionary and Glossary

Date ______________________

5. Knows to select the meaning which fits best according to the context in which the word is used

Mastery __________

DIRECTIONS: Read the sentences, paying close attention to the underlined word and the definition below the sentences. Then on the line in front of the number indicate the meaning which fits best according to the context of the sentence.

_____ 1. The Indians pounded the corn into meal.

_____ 2. Kathryn prepared a delicious meal for her sisters.
- a. breakfast, lunch, dinner
- b. grain ground up
- c. dry and powdery

_____ 3. I tire easily.

_____ 4. Marguerite's bicycle had a flat tire.
- a. ring of rubber that is filled around the rim of a wheel
- b. boring
- c. make weary

_____ 5. The shot woke me up.

_____ 6. Greg is a good shot.
- a. breath
- b. sound made by a weapon
- c. person who shoots

_____ 7. The barge moved slowly up the river.

_____ 8. Glen will barge through the door any minute now.
- a. flat-bottom boat used for freight
- b. interrupt in a clumsy, rude manner
- c. a crowd

_____ 9. As Louise spoke, she stroked the cat.

_____ 10. The stroke of the clock frightened the burglar.
- a. a sound of a striking clock
- b. action
- c. to caress with the hand

_____ 11. Kathryn is a brave person.

_____ 12. The braves were on the warpath.
- a. Indian warrior
- b. having courage
- c. shortstop

II. WORD ATTACK SKILLS C. Uses Dictionary and Glossary 6. Knows the meaning and use of guide words

OBJECTIVE: The pupil will demonstrate a knowledge of the meaning and use of guide words.

DIRECTIONS: Carefully study the list of words and the dictionary guide words. Now match each word with thc correct guide words by writing the letter of the guide words in front of the dictionary word.

l	1.	mine	a.	caribou-carrot
f	2.	bread	b.	refuse-regret
h	3.	odds	c.	cedar-cement
b	4.	regard	d.	domicile-door
g	5.	tarry	e.	shelf-shield
i	6.	manikin	f.	brave-breath
e	7.	shelter	g.	tare-task
d	8.	domino	h.	octabe-odor
c	9.	celery	i.	manganese-manito
a	10.	carnival	j.	taste-teach
			k.	sink-siren
			l.	miller-mince

MASTERY REQUIREMENT: 8 correct responses

Indicate mastery on the student response sheet with a check.

FOURTH LEVEL

II. WORD ATTACK SKILLS

Name ______________________

C. Uses Dictionary and Glossary

Date ______________________

6. Knows the meaning and use of guide words

Mastery __________

DIRECTIONS: Carefully study the list of words on the left and the dictionary guide words. Now match each word with the correct guide words by writing the letter of the guide word in front of the dictionary word.

____	1.	mine	a.	caribou-carrot
____	2.	bread	b.	refuse-regret
____	3.	odds	c.	cedar-cement
____	4.	regard	d.	domicile-door
____	5.	tarry	e.	shelf-shield
____	6.	manikin	f.	brave-breath
____	7.	shelter	g.	tare-task
____	8.	domino	h.	octabe-odor
____	9.	celery	i.	manganese-manito
____	10.	carnival	j.	taste-teach
			k.	sink-siren
			l.	miller-mince

FOURTH LEVEL

II. WORD ATTACK SKILLS **C. Uses Dictionary and Glossary** **7. Knows the meaning and use of the secondary accent mark**

OBJECTIVE: The pupil will demonstrate knowledge of the meaning and use of the secondary accent mark.

DIRECTIONS: Study the words in the list and the phonetic spelling and accent marks for each word. Pronounce these words to your teacher. Check the word when the student pronounces it correctly.

____	1.	reenforce	rē′ en fôrs′
____	2.	penicillin	pen′ ə sil′ən
____	3.	escalator	es′ kə lā′ tər
____	4.	disavow	dis′ ə vou′
____	5.	primary	pri′ mer′ ē
____	6.	dictionary	dik′ shən er′ē
____	7.	artificial	är′ tə fish′ əl
____	8.	nectarine	nek′ tər ēn′
____	9.	discoloration	dis kul′ ər ā′ shən
____	10.	necessary	nes′ ə ser′ē

MASTERY REQUIREMENT: 8 correct response

Indicate mastery on the student response sheet with a check.

FOURTH LEVEL

II. WORD ATTACK SKILLS

C. Uses Dictionary and Glossary

7. Knows the meaning and use of the secondary accent mark

Name ______________________

Date ______________________

Mastery __________

DIRECTIONS: Study the words in the list and the phonetic spelling and accent marks for each word. Pronounce these words to your teacher.

____	1.	reenforce	rē´ en fôrs´
____	2.	penicillin	pen´ ə sil´ən
____	3.	escalator	es´ kə lā´ tər
____	4.	disavow	dis´ ə vou´
____	5.	primary	pri´ mer´ ē
____	6.	dictionary	dik´ shən er´ē
____	7.	artificial	är´ tə fish´ əl
____	8.	nectarine	nek´ tər ēn´
____	9.	discoloration	dis kul´ ər ā´ shən
____	10.	necessary	nes´ ə ser´ē

FOURTH LEVEL

III. COMPREHENSION A. Finding the Main Idea 1. Choosing title for material read

OBJECTIVE: The pupil will demonstrate the ability to choose titles for material read.

DIRECTIONS: Read the selection and place an X in front of the title that is most appropriate.

1. Do you like to play? Do you go to school with kids who like to play games? Playing games together is a way of sharing fun, time, and joy. Playing can be fun for everybody when everyone tries hard and is active. Even grown-ups enjoy playing games.

    ____ a. Playing Is For Kids
    _x_ b. Playing Games
    ____ c. Grown-Up Play

2. Some old-timers are good weather forecasters. They don't use any fangle dangle equipment or expensive tools. These weather-wise people use their eyes, ears, nose, and the feeling in their bones. The sky, birds, trees and a thousand other little things all around us help those old-timers to correctly predict storms, clear skies, and sunny days.

    ____ a. Equipment for Weather Forecasting
    ____ b. Sky, Birds, and Trees
    _x_ c. Old-Timers as Weather Forecasters

3. Did you know that there are 100 different kinds of palm? There are the coconut palm, the sage palm, the African palm, and the date palm to name but a few. Each of these is found in different areas dependent on the moisture of the land. Some palms need more water than other kinds of palms. The date palm can grow in very dry areas.

    _x_ a. Palm Trees
    ____ b. Moisture
    ____ c. Date Palms

4. A thrilling experience is to stand in front of the United Nations headquarters in New York and look at the many flags flurrying in the breeze. Every member of the United Nations has its national emblem crackling in the wind. National flags tell the rich and inspiring story of every country. Every color, symbol, word, or stripe expresses the sentiment, the folklore, and the history of a nation.

    _x_ a. Flags Are National Emblems
    ____ b. Colors and Stripes
    ____ c. United Nations

MASTERY REQUIREMENT: 3 correct responses

Indicate mastery on the student response sheet with a check.

FOURTH LEVEL

III. COMPREHENSION

A. Finding the Main Idea

1. Choosing titles for material read

Name ______________________________

Date ______________________________

Mastery __________

DIRECTIONS: Read the selections and place an X in front of the title that is most appropriate.

1. Do you like to play? Do you go to school with kids who like to play games? Playing games together is a way of sharing fun, time, and joy. Playing can be fun for everybody when everyone tries hard and is active. Even grown-ups enjoy playing games.

   _____ a. Playing Is For Kids
   _____ b. Playing Games
   _____ c. Grown-Up Play

2. Some old-timers are good weather forecasters. They don't use any fangle dangle equipment or expensive tools. These weather-wise people use their eyes, ears, nose, and the feelings in their bones. The sky, birds, trees and a thousand other little things all around us help those old-timers to correctly predict storms, clear skies, and sunny days.

   _____ a. Equipment for Weather Forecasting
   _____ b. Sky, Birds, and Trees
   _____ c. Old-Timers as Weather Forecasters

3. Did you know that there are 100 different kinds of palm? There are the coconut palm, the sage palm, the African palm, and the date palm to name but a few. Each of these is found in different areas dependent on the moisture of the land. Some palms need more water than other kinds of palms. The date palm can grow in very dry areas.

   _____ a. Palm Trees
   _____ b. Moisture
   _____ c. Date Palms

4. A thrilling experience is to stand in front of the United Nations headquarters in New York and look at the many flags flurrying in the breeze. Every member of the United Nations has its national emblem crackling in the wind. National flags tell the rich and inspiring story of every country. Every color, symbol, word, or stripe expresses the sentiment, the folklore, and the history of a nation.

   _____ a. Flags Are National Emblems
   _____ b. Colors and Stripes
   _____ c. United Nations

FOURTH LEVEL

III. COMPREHENSION A. Finding the Main Idea 2. Can identify key words and topic sentences

OBJECTIVE: The pupil will demonstrate the ability to identify key words and topic sentences.

DIRECTIONS: Read each paragraph. On the line under the paragraph write the topic sentence.

1. Marguerite loved the different sounds of the petting zoo: cows mooing, geese honking, sheep baaing, pigs oinking, donkeys braying. She also loved the feel, the softness of a kitten, the hard shell of the turtle, the fuzziness of a baby chick, the smoothness of the horse. It could be said that Marguerite loved everything about the petting zoo.

   Marguerite loved everything about the petting zoo.

2. Eggs come in many sizes. Some eggs are large, some are medium size, and some are very small. Everyone knows the size of a chicken egg—but insects also lay eggs. Some of the smallest insects lay eggs that are so small that it would take one hundred eggs to make one inch. The housefly's egg in comparison is much bigger. It takes 25 housefly's eggs to make one inch.

   Eggs come in many sizes.

3. My dog became ill after eating meat balls. My dad and I had to take him to the veterinarian. The veterinarian had to pump out my dog's stomach. We left the dog at the Dog Clinic overnight. When my dad and I returned to get my dog, the veterinarian said that my dog barked with an Italian accent.

   My dog became ill after eating meat balls.

4. John Jacob Astor, fur trader, merchant, and investor in Manhattan real estate, had a humble beginning. He was born in Germany, the fourth son of a butcher. His mother was hard-working and saving. However, the family was frequently in want.

   John Jacob Astor had a humble beginning.

MASTERY REQUIREMENT: 3 correct responses

Indicate mastery on the student response sheet with a check.

FOURTH LEVEL

III. COMPREHENSION **Name** ______________________

A. Finding the Main Idea

Date ______________________

2. Can identify key words and topic sentences

Mastery ___________

DIRECTIONS: Read each paragraph. On the line under the paragraph write the topic sentence.

1. Marguerite loved the different sounds of the petting zoo: cows mooing, geese honking, sheep baaing, pigs oinking, donkeys braying. She also loved the feel, the softness of a kitten, the hard shell of the turtle, the fuzziness of a baby chick, the smoothness of the horse. It could be said that Marguerite loved everything about the petting zoo.

____

2. Eggs come in many sizes. Some eggs are large, some are medium size, and some are very small. Everyone knows the size of a chicken egg—but insects also lay eggs. Some of the smallest insects lay eggs that are so small that it would take one hundred eggs to make one inch. The housefly's egg in comparison is much bigger. It takes 25 housefly's eggs to make one inch.

____

3. My dog became ill after eating meat balls. My dad and I had to take him to the veterinarian. The veterinarian had to pump out my dog's stomach. We left the dog at the Dog Clinic overnight. When my dad and I returned to get my dog, the veterinarian said that my dog barked with an Italian accent.

____

4. John Jacob Astor, fur trader, merchant, and investor in Manhattan real estate, had a humble beginning. He was born in Germany, the fourth son of a butcher. His mother was hardworking and saving. However, the family was frequently in want.

____

FOURTH LEVEL

III. COMPREHENSION A. Finding the Main Idea 3. Summarizing

OBJECTIVE: The pupil will demonstrate the ability to summarize.

DIRECTIONS: Read the selection carefully. On the line below each paragraph summarize the selection in one sentence.

1. The strong, healthy lad of about seventeen, with enough schooling to permit him to read, write, and cipher, and with a crown or two in his pocket, started afoot for the city. On his way, he sat down under a tree and rested. While resting, he made three resolutions–to be honest, to be industrious, and to be fair. By the time the lad reached the city . . .

   A lad on his way to the city made three resolutions.

2. The man was described as stout and square-built, about five feet nine inches in height, with a high, square forehead and somewhat heavy features. He was good natured. His handwriting was wretched as was his spelling and grammar.

   The stout man was a poor writer.

3. Roger Williams–London bred, scholar, dreamer, and frontier scout. He founded Providence Rhode Island, and fought a fight for freedom.He is known for what we today call the American way of life. He believed in freedom and liberty, and equality both in law and government.

   Roger Williams fought for the American way of life or liberty and equality.

4. Pastoralists are a group of people who depend chiefly on herding as a way of life. They lead their herds from grassy area to grassy area. A pastoralist depends totally on animals and their care for his livelihood. As a group of people they do little or no farming and any vegetables in their diet are obtained by trading with farming people.

   Pastoralists depend totally on animals for a way of life.

MASTERY REQUIREMENT: 3 correct responses

Indicate mastery on the student response sheet with a check.

FOURTH LEVEL

III. COMPREHENSION

A. Finding the Main Idea

3. Summarizing

Name ______________________

Date ______________________

Mastery __________

DIRECTIONS: Read the selection carefully. On the line below each paragraph summarize the selection in one sentence.

1. The strong, healthy lad of about seventeen, with enough schooling to permit him to read, write, and cipher, and with a crown or two in his pocket, started afoot for the city. On his way, he sat down under a tree and rested. While resting, he made three resolutions–to be honest, to be industrious, and to be fair. By the time the lad reached the city . . .

____

2. The man was described as stout and square-built, about five feet nine inches in height, with a high square forehead and somewhat heavy features. He was good natured. His handwriting was wretched as was his spelling and grammar.

____

3 Roger Williams–London bred, scholar, dreamer, and frontier scout. He founded Providence, Rhode Island, and fought a fight for freedom. He is known for what we today call the American way of life. He believed in freedom and liberty, and equality both in law and government.

____

4. Pastoralists are a group of people who depend chiefly on herding as a way of life. They lead their herds from grassy area to grassy area. A pastoralist depends totally on animals and their care for his livelihood. As a group of people they do little or no farming and any vegetables in their diet are obtained by trading with farming people.

____

FOURTH LEVEL

III. COMPREHENSION B. Finding Details 1. Finding specific information

OBJECTIVE: The pupil will demonstrate the ability to find specific information.

DIRECTIONS: Read the following selection carefully. Answer the questions at the end of the selection.

The Natchez Trace ran from the old Cumberland settlements to the rich and rowdy city of Natchez on the Mississippi River. History books record the opening of the Trace to the company of Don Hernando de Soto. It is described as the oldest road in the world and the one having the most colorful history.

Traders, hunters, traitors, soldiers, fortune hunters, and preachers traveled the Trace. The Trace was romantic but harsh, wild, and cruel. There was much bloodshed along this road. The road was narrow, rough, and dangerous. For some, the road meant heartbreak, death, and murder. For others, it brought joy, wealth, fame, love, and satisfaction.

The Trace was killed in the 1830's by the spark showers of the steamboat. Riding the steamboat down the Mississippi River was cheaper, faster, more comfortable, and fancier than horseback in the wilderness. The road may be dead but its history lingers on.

1. What two places did the Natchez Trace connect?

   Cumberland settlements and Natchez

2. Who were said to have been the first men to travel the Trace?

   Hernando do Soto and his men

3. Name several groups of people who traveled this road?

   traders, hunters, farmers, mail riders, preachers, fortune hunters

4. Use three words to describe the road.

   narrow, rough, dangerous

5. What killed the Trace?

   steamboat

6. Why did the Trace die?

   steamboat travel was cheaper, faster, and more comfortable

MASTERY REQUIREMENT: 5 correct responses

Indicate mastery on the student response sheet with a check.

FOURTH LEVEL

III. COMPREHEHSION

B. Finding Details

1. Finding specific information

Name ______________________

Date ______________________

Mastery __________

DIRECTIONS: Read the following selection carefully. Answer the questions at the end of the selection.

The Natchez Trace ran from the old Cumberland settlements to the rich and rowdy city of Natchez on the Mississippi River. History books record the opening of the Trace to the company of Don Hernando de Soto. It is described as the oldest road in the world and the one having the most colorful history.

Traders, hunters, traitors, soldiers, fortune hunters, and preachers traveled the Trace. The Trace was romantic but harsh, wild, and cruel. There was much bloodshed along this road. The road was narrow, rough, and dangerous. For some, the road meant heartbreak, death, and murder. For others, it brought joy, wealth, fame, love, and satisfaction.

The Trace was killed in the 1830's by the spark showers of the steamboat. Riding the steamboat down the Mississippi River was cheaper, faster, more comfortable, and fancier than horseback in the wilderness. The road may be dead but its history lingers on.

1. What two places did the Natchez Trace connect?

____

2. Who were said to have been the first men to travel the Trace?

____

3. Name several groups of people who traveled this road?

____

4. Use three words to describe the road.

____

5. What killed the Trace?

____

6. Why did the Trace die?

____

FOURTH LEVEL

III. COMPREHENSION B. Finding Details 2. Interpreting descriptive words and phrases

OBJECTIVE: The pupil will demonstrate the ability to interpret descriptive words and phrases.

DIRECTIONS: Read the sentences carefully. Place an X in front of the best meaning of the underlined descriptive words or phrases.

1. The howling wind and pounding rain battered the old man as he walked home.

   _____ a. the cyclone
   _____ b. the calm day
   __x__ c. the storm

2. The family reunion featured dinner on the grounds.

   _____ a. people ate off the ground
   __x__ b. dinner was eaten outdoors
   _____ c. dinner was not served

3. The politician was barking up the wrong tree when he asked me to vote for him.

   __x__ a. the listener was not friendly to the politician
   _____ b. the politician was a dog
   _____ c. the politician was hunting

4. Nyette was as happy as a lark.

   __x__ a. very happy
   _____ b. singing
   _____ c. chirping

5. Kathryn was on top of the world when she learned that her cake won a blue ribbon at the fair.

   _____ a. on one foot
   __x__ b. feeling pleased and happy
   _____ c. flying

6. Eddie is as sly as a fox.

   __x__ a. sneaky, deceptive
   _____ b. has a bushy tail
   _____ c. looks like a fox

7. Cool as a cucumber describes Sam.

   __x__ a. calm and smooth
   _____ b. cold
   _____ c. long and chubby

(Continued on page 140.)

FOURTH LEVEL

III. COMPREHENSION

B. Finding Details

2. Interpreting descriptive words and phrases

Name ______________________________

Date ______________________________

Mastery ___________

DIRECTIONS: Read the sentences carefully. Place an X in front of the best meaning of the underlined descriptive words or phrases.

1. The howling wind and pounding rain battered the old man as he walked home.

_____ a. the cyclone
_____ b. the calm day
_____ c. the storm

2. The family reunion featured dinner on the grounds.

_____ a. people ate off the ground
_____ b. dinner was eaten outdoors
_____ c. dinner was not served

3. The politician was barking up the wrong tree when he asked me to vote for him.

_____ a. the listener was not friendly to the politician
_____ b. the politician was a dog
_____ c. the politician was hunting

4. Nyette was as happy as a lark.

_____ a. very happy
_____ b. singing
_____ c. chirping

5. Kathryn was on top of the world when she learned that her cake won a blue ribbon at the fair.

_____ a. on one foot
_____ b. feeling pleased and happy
_____ c. flying

6. Eddie is as sly as a fox.

_____ a. sneaky, deceptive
_____ b. has a bushy tail
_____ c. looks like a fox

(Continued)

8. Her smile was as sweet as honey.

____ a. tasted good
__x__ b. pleasing
____ c. don't know

MASTERY REQUIREMENT: 6 correct responses

Indicate mastery on the student response sheet with a check.

7. Cool as a cucumber describes Sam.

_____ a. calm and smooth
_____ b. cold
_____ c. long and chubby

8. Her smile was as sweet as honey.

_____ a. tasted good
_____ b. pleasing
_____ c. don't know

FOURTH LEVEL

III. COMPREHENSION   B. Finding Details   3. Selecting facts to remember

OBJECTIVE: The pupil will demonstrate the ability to select facts to remember.

DIRECTIONS: Read the selection very carefully. Then cover the paragraphs and answer the questions, remembering what you have just read.

On Monday night, July 31, 1978, Pete Rose, a third baseman for the Cincinnati Reds, extended his consecutive game hitting streak. The eyes and ears of the baseball world were on Pete Rose as the game between the Reds and the Braves was played in Atlanta, Georgia.

Millions watching television, thousands listening to radios, the full stadium, and everyone who loves America's number one pastime were hoping for an eyeful or an earful. Would the Cincinnati star hit again? Which inning would it be? What kind of a hit would it be?

Pete Rose did get a hit, which raised his hitting streak to 44 hits, a record tie in the National League. The hit was a ground-ball single to the right field at the top of the sixth inning. This hit tied Rose with Willis Keele (1897) for the longest streak in National League history. The crowd of 45,000 plus gave Rose a standing ovation of almost two minutes.

Rose started his hitting streak on June 14. He is a dozen games away from Joe DiMaggio's record of 56 hits with the New York Yankees in 1941. Will he reach that goal this year? How long will the hitting streak last? It ended at 44. Maybe another hitting streak will begin soon.

1. Who? Pete Rose

2. What? Hitting streak of 44 hits

3. Where? Atlanta, Georgia

4. When? July 31, 1978

5. How? A hit in the sixth inning

MASTERY REQUIREMENT: Full correct answers

Indicate mastery on the student response sheet with a check.

FOURTH LEVEL

III. COMPREHENSION

B. Finding Details

3. Selecting facts to remember

Name ______________________________

Date ______________________________

Mastery____________

DIRECTIONS: Read the selection carefully. Then cover the paragraphs and answer the questions, remembering what you have just read.

On Monday night, July 31, 1978, Pete Rose, a third baseman for the Cincinnati Reds, extended his consecutive game hitting streak. The eyes and ears of the baseball world were on Pete Rose as the game between the Reds and the Braves was played in Atlanta, Georgia.

Millions watching television, thousands listening to radios, the full stadium, and everyone who loves America's number one pastime were hoping for an eyeful or an earful. Would the Cincinnati star hit again? Which inning would it be? What kind of a hit would it be?

Pete Rose did get a hit, which raised his hitting streak to 44 hits, a record tie in the National League. The hit was a ground-ball single to the right field at the top of the sixth inning. This hit tied Rose with Willis Keele (1897) for the longest streak in National League history. The crowd of 45,000 plus gave Rose a standing ovation of almost two minutes.

Rose started his hitting streak on June 14. He is a dozen games away from Joe DiMaggio's record of 56 hits with the New York Yankees in 1941. Will he reach that goal this year? How long will the hitting streak last? It ended at 44. Maybe another hitting streak will begin soon.

1. Who? ______________________________

2. What? ______________________________

3. Where? ______________________________

4. When? ______________________________

5. How? ______________________________

FOURTH LEVEL

III. COMPREHENSION B. Finding Details 4. Selecting facts to support main idea

OBJECTIVE: The pupil will demonstrate the ability to select facts to support the main idea of a selection.

DIRECTIONS: Read very carefully the paragraphs below. Select the facts that support the main idea of each paragraph.

Movie star, rent-a-car super-salesman, football jersey 32, tremendous football player, exciting person—all these things are one human being. This person is O. J. Simpson, a San Francisco 49ers football player, frequently known as "Juice." O. J. Simpson, also known as O. J. in the sports world, began his professional football career with the Buffalo Bills of New York. He was traded to the San Francisco 49ers. He earns nearly $50,000 a week. At the age of 31, after a career with the Buffalo Bills in which he once gained 2,003 yards in one season, he is with a team that plans to throw him the ball more.

O. J. played football in junior college as well as in senior college. He won many awards as a member of the University of Southern California Trojans. His coaches knew he was an outstanding runner and planned the game strategy around his skills.

The 49ers' game strategy is to use O. J. as a halfback in pass offense as well as on the ground. The coach would like to get the ball to O. J.'s hands about 25 times a game. He is thinking about 15 runs and 10 passes.

O. J. has olympian speed. His jersey will be red and white. Experts say that at 31, he's as good as he was at 28. Wherever he goes he gains much attention from his fans. He is one of the most popular American males.

Paragraph 1: Main idea O. J. Simpson
a. football player
b. super salesman
c. movie star

Paragraph 2: Main idea traded from Buffalo Bills to 49ers
a. salary, $50,000
b. runner
c. catches passes

Paragraph 3: Main idea football experience
a. junior college, senior college
b. won awards
c. outstanding runner

Paragraph 4: Main idea game strategy
a. halfback
b. pass offense
c. catch ball 25 times

Paragraph 5: Main idea qualities—olympian speed
a. good as he was at 28
b. gets much attention from fans
c. jersey is red and white

MASTERY REQUIREMENT: 12 correct responses

Indicate mastery on the student response sheet wth a check.

FOURTH LEVEL

III. COMPREHENSION

Name ____________________

B. Finding Details

Date ____________________

4. Selecting facts to support main idea

Mastery __________

DIRECTIONS: Read very carefully the paragraphs below. Select the facts that support the main idea of each paragraph.

Movie star, rent-a-car super-salesman, football jersey 32, tremendous football player, exciting person—all these things are one human being. This person is O. J. Simpson, a San Francisco 49ers football player, frequently known as "Juice." O. J. Simpson, also known as O. J. in the sports world, began his professional football career with the Buffalo Bills of New York. He was traded to the San Francisco 49ers. He earns nearly $50,000 a week. At the age of 31, after a career with the Buffalo Bills in which he once gained 2,003 yards in one season, he is with a team that plans to throw him the ball more.

O. J. played football in junior college as well as in senior college. He won many awards as a member of the University of Southern California Trojans. His coaches knew he was an outstanding runner and planned the game strategy around his skills.

The 49ers' game strategy is to use O. J. as a halfback in pass offense as well as on the ground. The coach would like to get the ball to O. J.'s hands about 25 times a game. He is thinking about 15 runs and 10 passes.

O. J. has olympian speed. His jersey will be red and white. Experts say that at 31, he's as good as he was at 28. Wherever he goes he gains much attention from his fans. He is one of the most popular American males.

Paragraph 1: Main idea ____________________
a. ____________________
b. ____________________
c. ____________________

Paragraph 2: Main idea ____________________
a. ____________________
b. ____________________
c. ____________________

Paragraph 3: Main idea ____________________
a. ____________________
b. ____________________
c. ____________________

Paragraph 4: Main idea ____________________
a. ____________________
b. ____________________
c. ____________________

Paragraph 5: Main idea ____________________
a. ____________________
b. ____________________
c. ____________________

FOURTH LEVEL

III. COMPREHENSION B. Finding Details 5. Using study guides, charts, outlines

OBJECTIVE: The pupil will demonstrate the ability to use study guides, charts, and outlines.

DIRECTIONS: Study the three boxes carefully. Answer the questions by telling where you would find the correct answers.

Box A–Outline

I. Kinds of Airplanes
   A. Helicopters
   B. Jet propelled
   C. Gliders
   D. Engine propelled

Box B–Study Guide

12 inches	=	1 foot
3 feet	=	1 yard
36 inches	=	1 yard
5,280 feet	=	1 mile
1,760 yards	=	1 mile

Box C–Chart

Deep Fat Frying Temperatures

Kind of Food	*Temperature*	*Time*
Doughnuts	300-375°F	About 4 minutes
Croquettes	375-395°F	Until brown
Fish cakes	375-390°F	Until brown
Oysters	400-450°F	2 minutes
French fried potatoes	350-395°F	About 3 minutes

1. How many feet in a mile? Box B or Study Guide
2. When was the helicopter invented? Box A or Outline
3. Who designed the first engine propelled plane? Box A or Outline
4. How long must you deep fry croquettes? Box C or Chart
5. What temperature is needed to fry potatoes? Box C or Chart
6. How many inches in a yard? Box B or Study Guide
7. Which plane is used for short distances? Box A or Outline
8. Which food requires a temperature of 400°F for frying? Box C or Chart
9. How much time is required to fry fish cakes? Box C or Chart
10. Where would you find the number of feet in a mile? Box B or Study Guide

MASTERY REQUIREMENT: 8 correct responses

Indicate mastery on the student response sheet with a check.

FOURTH LEVEL

III. COMPREHENSION

B. Finding Details

5. Using study guides, charts, outlines

Name ______________________

Date ______________________

Mastery __________

DIRECTIONS: Study the three boxes carefully. Answer the questions by telling where you would find the correct answers.

Box A–Outline

I. Kinds of airplanes
   A. Helicopters
   B. Jet propelled
   C. Gliders
   D. Engine propelled

Box B–Study Guide

12 inches	=	1 foot
3 feet	=	1 yard
36 inches	=	1 yard
5,280 feet	=	1 mile
1,760 yards	=	1 mile

Box C–Chart

Deep Fat Frying Temperatures

Kind of Food	*Temperature*	*Time*
Doughnuts	300-375°F	About 4 minutes
Croquettes	375-395°F	Until brown
Fish cakes	375-390°F	Until brown
Oysters	400-450°F	2 minutes
French fried potatoes	350-395°F	About 3 minutes

1. How many feet in a mile? ______________________
2. When was the helicopter invented? ______________________
3. Who designed the first engine propelled plane? ______________________
4. How long must you deep fry croquettes? ______________________
5. What temperature is needed to fry potatoes? ______________________
6. How many inches in a yard? ______________________
7. Which plane is used for short distances? ______________________
8. Which food requires a temperature of 400°F for frying? ______________________
9. How much time is required to fry fish cakes? ______________________
10. Where would you find the number of feet in a mile? ______________________

FOURTH LEVEL

III. COMPREHENSION B. Finding Details 6. Verifying answers

OBJECTIVE: The pupil will demonstrate the ability to verify answers.

DIRECTIONS: Read the selection. Read the statements that follow and indicate which line verifies the statement. Write the line number on the line in front of the statement.

Directions for ICE CREAM

To insure good frozen desserts it is necessary to use the best ingredients, the ice and salt in the right proportions,and to freeze at the proper rate of speed.

Always boil sugar and water together to a syrup for water ices, as this melts the sugar thoroughly and gives body to the ices.

When cream is the foundation for the dessert, scald it, and add the sugar to the scalding cream.

In the preparation of ice cream, after the freezer can is in place, filled, and the ice and salt packed around it, let the mixture stand about five minutes; then turn the crank steadily, but not too fast, for the first few moments, afterwards increasing the speed till the freezing is completed. Then remove the dasher and scrape the mixture from the sides of the can, packing it down firmly. Replace the top of the can and cover with more ice. Put a piece of carpet or other heavy material over all, and stand aside for the mixture to ripen.

Rumford Complete Cookbook, 1929

9	1.	Ice and salt must be packed around the freezer can.
5	2.	Sugar and water are boiled to melt the sugar.
2	3.	To get good desserts, it is important to use good ingredients.
15	4.	Cover the can of ice cream with more ice and a piece of carpet when finished.
11	5.	When cranking the ice freezer begin cranking slowly.
3	6.	Rate of speed when freezing ice cream is important.
6	7.	Scalded cream is used in some desserts.
10	8.	Turn the crank after the mixture has stood for about five minutes.
12	9.	The dasher is scraped after the ice cream is made.
15	10.	One must wait a few minutes after mixing the ice cream before eating it.

MASTERY REQUIREMENT: 8 correct responses

Indicate mastery on the student response sheet with a check.

FOURTH LEVEL

III. COMPREHENSION

B. Finding Details

6. Verifying answers

Name ______________________

Date ______________________

Mastery __________

DIRECTIONS: Read the selection. Read the statements that follow and indicate which line verifies the statement. Write the line number on the line in front of the statement.

Directions for ICE CREAM

To insure good frozen desserts it is necessary to use the best ingredients, the ice and salt in the right proportions, and to freeze at the proper rate of speed.

Always boil sugar and water together to a syrup for water ices, as this melts the sugar thoroughly and gives body to the ices.

When cream is the foundation for the dessert, scald it, and add the sugar to the scalding cream.

In the preparation of ice cream, after the freezer can is in place, filled, and the ice and salt packed around it, let the mixture stand about five minutes; then turn the crank steadily, but not too fast, for the first few moments, afterwards increasing the speed till the freezing is completed. Then remove the dasher and scrape the mixture from the sides of the can, packing it down firmly. Replace the top of the can and cover with more ice. Put a piece of carpet or other heavy material over all, and stand aside for the mixture to ripen.

Rumford Complete Cookbook, 1929

_____ 1. Ice and salt must be packed around the freezer can.

_____ 2. Sugar and water are boiled to melt the sugar.

_____ 3. To get good desserts, it is important to use good ingredients.

_____ 4. Cover the can of ice cream with more ice and a piece of carpet when finished.

_____ 5. When cranking the ice freezer begin cranking slowly.

_____ 6. Rate of speed when freezing ice cream is important.

_____ 7. Scalded cream is used in some desserts.

_____ 8. Turn the crank after the mixture has stood for about five minutes.

_____ 9. The dasher is scraped after the ice cream is made.

_____ 10. One must wait a few minutes after mixing the ice cream before eating it.

FOURTH LEVEL

III. COMPREHENSION B. Finding Details 7. Arranging ideas in sequence

OBJECTIVE: The pupil will demonstrate the ability to arrange ideas in sequence.

DIRECTIONS: Read the following phrases and place them in correct sequence. Do so by placing numbers 1, 2, 3, 4, 5, or 6 in the front of each phrase.

Morning:

5 a. Napped after lunch
1 b. Made breakfast
2 c. Got everyone off to school
3 d. Made beds
4 e. Had lunch

Afternoon:

1 a. Went shopping for groceries before school let out
3 b. Gave kids a snack after school
2 c. Picked kids up at school
4 d. Began dinner
6 e. After dinner, washed the dishes
5 f. While still making dinner, put in a load of wash

Evening:

1 a. Urged the kids to begin homework
4 b. Went to bed
2 c. Folded laundry and watched television
3 d. Checked kids' homework, another load of laundry

MASTERY REQUIREMENT: 12 correct responses

Indicate mastery on the student response sheet with a check.

FOURTH LEVEL

III. COMPREHENSION

B. Finding Details

7. Arranging ideas in sequence

Name ______________________

Date ______________________

Mastery ___________

DIRECTIONS: Read the following phrases and place them in correct sequence. Do so by placing numbers 1, 2, 3, 4, 5, or 6 in the front of each phrase.

Morning:

_____ a. Napped after lunch

_____ b. Made breakfast

_____ c. Got everyone off to school

_____ d. Made beds

_____ e. Had lunch

Afternoon:

_____ a. Went shopping for groceries before school let out

_____ b. Gave kids a snack after school

_____ c. Picked kids up at school

_____ d. Began dinner

_____ e. After dinner, washed the dishes

_____ f. While still making dinner, put in a load of wash

Evening:

_____ a. Urged the kids to begin homework

_____ b. Went to bed

_____ c. Folded laundry and watched television

_____ d. Checked kids'homework, another load of laundry

FOURTH LEVEL

III. COMPREHENSION C. Creative Reading 1. Able to interpret story ideas (generalize)

OBJECTIVE: The pupil will demonstrate the ability to interpret story ideas.

DIRECTIONS: Read each paragraph very carefully. Then place an X in front of the phrase that interprets the ideas of the paragraph.

1. There is nothing new about denim. History tells us that the original denim was produced as serge in Nimes, France, and called Serge de Nimes. That is where the name comes from—de nim. The fabric was said to have been worn both by the poor and the wealthy.

    ____ a. Serge de Nimes is a place in France
    __x__ b. The history of denim is a long one
    ____ c. Denim is worn only by teenagers
    ____ d. Denim is a soft fabric

2. It is said that Levi Strauss arrived in California during the Gold Rush of 1850 with many bolts of denim. Levi intended to sell the fabric for tents. Shortly after arriving, he discovered that the gold miners were not interested in a strong fabric for tents but rather they needed pants that would last a long time. So, he took the denim material and made pants.

    ____ a. Levi Strauss was a gold miner
    __x__ b. Levi Strauss was a clever man
    ____ c. Levi Strauss bought the first denim tent
    ____ d. Gold Rush of California was in 1850

3. So you want to be an Olympic star and win a gold medal. You can. If you really want to do something, and you are willing to work very, very hard, you can do those things you dream about. Now it won't happen overnight or next week or next month. To be a success, first you have to have the desire.

    ____ a. Hard work will win you a gold medal
    ____ b. Everyone should dream a little
    ____ c. Olympic stars win gold medals
    __x__ d. The first step to success is to have the desire

4. Olympic champions are very proud of their medals. The medals are won only after a great deal of hard work. To get to the Olympics, millions of young men and women start training at a young age. It is not unusual for a runner or diver or swimmer to train between two and eight hours a day. It takes a lot of time and practice, practice, practice.

    ____ a. All Olympic participants win medals
    ____ b. Only men take part in the Olympics
    __x__ c. Olympic champions must spend a great deal of time in training
    ____ d. It's easy to win a gold medal

MASTERY REQUIREMENT: 3 correct responses

Indicate mastery on the student response sheet with a check.

FOURTH LEVEL

III. COMPREHENSIVE

C. Creative Reading

1. Able to interpret story ideas

Name ______________________________

Date ______________________________

Mastery __________

DIRECTIONS: Read each paragraph very carefully. Then place an X in front of the phrase that interprets the idea of the paragraph.

1. There is nothing new about denim. History tells us that the original denim was produced as serge in Nimes, France, and called Serge de Nimes. That is where the name comes from—de nim. The fabric was said to have been worn both by the poor and the wealthy.

_____ a. Serge de Nimes is a place in France
_____ b. The history of denim is a long one
_____ c. Denim is worn only by teenagers
_____ d. Denim is a soft fabric

2. It is said that Levi Strauss arrived in California during the Gold Rush of 1850 with many bolts of denim. Levi intended to sell the fabric for tents. Shortly after arriving, he discovered that the gold miners were not interested in a strong fabric for tents but rather they needed pants that would last a long time. So, he took the denim material and made pants.

_____ a. Levi Strauss was a gold miner
_____ b. Levi Strauss was a clever man
_____ c. Levi Strauss bought the first denim tent
_____ d. Gold Rush of California was in 1850

3. So you want to be an Olympic star and win a gold medal. You can. If you really want to do something, and you are willing to work very, very hard, you can do those things you dream about. Now it won't happen overnight or next week or next month. To be a success, first you have to have the desire.

_____ a. Hard work will win you a gold medal
_____ b. Everyone should dream a little
_____ c. Olympic stars win gold medals
_____ d. The first step to success is to have the desire

4. Olympic champions are very proud of their medals. The medals are won only after a great deal of hard work. To get to the Olympics, millions of young men and women start training at a young age. It is not unusual for a runner or diver or swimmer to train between two and eight hours a day. It takes a lot of time and practice, practice, practice.

_____ a. All Olympic participants win medals
_____ b. Only men take part in the Olympics
_____ c. Olympic champions must spend a great deal of time in training
_____ d. It's easy to win a gold medal

FOURTH LEVEL

III. COMPREHENSION   C. Creative Reading   2. Able to see relationships

OBJECTIVE: The pupil will demonstrate the ability to see relationships.

DIRECTIONS: Read the paragraphs very carefully. Place an X in front of the time (present, past, or future) that you think this event probably took place.

1. The coach rocked along the bumpy road for many hours before reaching the inn where the passengers were to spend the night.

    _____ a. Present
    __x__ b. Past
    _____ c. Future

2. The advertisement read, breakfast in California, lunch in London, and dinner in New York all within twenty-four hours.

    _____ a. Present
    _____ b. Past
    __x__ c. Future

3. Driving fifty-five miles an hour down the interstate, Kathryn was enjoying her new automobile.

    __x__ a. Present
    _____ b. Past
    _____ c. Future

4. The king scolded his queen for wearing her new dress one inch above her ankle.

    _____ a. Present
    __x__ b. Past
    _____ c. Future

5. The satellite permitted the TV viewers to witness the Bolshoi Ballet as they performed in Moscow.

    __x__ a. Present
    _____ b. Past
    _____ c. Future

6. The rocket landed on Venus and the passengers were greeted with much warmth by the planet's inhabitants.

    _____ a. Present
    _____ b. Past
    __x__ c. Future

7. With a flick of a switch, dinner was prepared, cooked and the table set.

    _____ a. Present
    _____ b. Past
    __x__ c. Future

(Continued on page 156)

FOURTH LEVEL

III. COMPREHENSION

C. Creative Reading

2. Able to see relationships

Name ______________________

Date ______________________

Mastery __________

DIRECTIONS: Read the paragraphs very carefully. Place an X in front of the time (present, past, future) that you think this event probably took place.

1. The coach rocked along the bumpy road for many hours before reaching the inn where the passengers were to spend the night.

____ a. Present
____ b. Past
____ c. Future

2. The advertisement read, breakfast in California, lunch in London, and dinner in New York all within twenty-four hours.

____ a. Present
____ b. Past
____ c. Future

3. Driving fifty-five miles an hour down the interstate, Kathryn was enjoying her new automobile.

____ a. Present
____ b. Past
____ c. Future

4. The king scolded his queen for wearing her new dress one inch above her ankle.

____ a. Present
____ b. Past
____ c. Future

5. The satellite permitted the TV viewers to witness the Bolshoi Ballet as they performed in Moscow.

____ a. Present
____ b. Past
____ c. Future

6. The rocket landed on Venus and the passengers were greeted with much warmth by the planet's inhabitants.

____ a. Present
____ b. Past
____ c. Future

(Continued)

8. The women stood over the black kettles and boiled the ingredients to make soup.

_____ a. Present
_x_ b. Past
_____ c. Future

9. Eddie's new automobile runs on an electric battery that needs recharging every 5,000 miles.

_____ a. Present
_____ b. Past
_x_ c. Future

10. Marguerite spent the night in the barn nursing her colt that had been struck by the Model T.

_____ a. Present
_x_ b. Past
_____ c. Future

MASTERY REQUIREMENT: 8 correct responses

Indicate mastery on the student response sheet with a check.

7. With a flick of a switch, dinner was prepared, cooked and the table set.

_____ a. Present
_____ b. Past
_____ c. Future

8. The women stood over the black kettles and boiled the ingredients to make soap.

_____ a. Present
_____ b. Past
_____ c. Future

9. Eddie's new automobile runs on an electric battery that needs recharging every 5,000 miles.

_____ a. Present
_____ b. Past
_____ c. Future

10. Marguerite spent the night in the barn nursing her colt that had been struck by the Model T.

_____ a. Present
_____ b. Past
_____ c. Future

FOURTH LEVEL

III. COMPREHENSION **C. Creative Reading** **3. Able to identify the mood of a reading selection**

OBJECTIVE: The pupil will demonstrate the ability to identify the mood of a reading selection.

DIRECTIONS: Read the sentences carefully. Place an X in front of the mood that the writer is projecting.

1. The room was filled with balloons, bright streamers, and the happy voices of many boys and girls.

   ____ 1. Friendly
   _x_ 2. Exciting
   ____ 3. Mysterious
   ____ 4. Frightening

2. Mother gave a deep sigh, closed her eyes for a brief second, and grasped the back of a chair for support.

   _x_ 1. Worry
   ____ 2. Happiness
   ____ 3. Anger
   ____ 4. Nervous

3. Quietly, Peggy walked into the dark castle and up the circular staircase to the room where the body was found.

   ____ 1. Friendly
   _x_ 2. Mysterious
   ____ 3. Happiness
   ____ 4. Anger

4. As Jessica left the room, the wind blew the shutter closed and the candle slowly flickered and went out.

   ____ 1. Anger
   ____ 2. Friendly
   ____ 3. Despair
   _x_ 4. Mysterious

5. The man ran up the stairs two at a time, shouting with ecstasy that he had won a million dollars.

   ____ 1. Sympathy
   ____ 2. Fear
   _x_ 3. Joy
   ____ 4. Anger

(Continued on page 160.)

FOURTH LEVEL

III. COMPREHENSION

C. Creative Reading

3. Able to identify the mood of a reading selection

Name ______________________________

Date ______________________________

Mastery ___________

DIRECTIONS: Read the sentences carefully. Place an X in front of the mood that the writer is projecting.

1. The room was filled with balloons, bright streamers, and the happy voices of many boys and girls.

_____ 1. Friendly
_____ 2. Exciting
_____ 3. Mysterious
_____ 4. Frightening

2. Mother gave a deep sigh, closed her eyes for a brief second, and grasped the back of a chair for support.

_____ 1. Worry
_____ 2. Happiness
_____ 3. Anger
_____ 4. Nervous

3. Quietly, Peggy walked into the dark castle and up the circular staircase to the room where the body was found.

_____ 1. Friendly
_____ 2. Mysterious
_____ 3. Happiness
_____ 4. Anger

4. As Jessica left the room, the wind blew the shutter closed and the candle slowly flickered and went out.

_____ 1. Anger
_____ 2. Friendly
_____ 3. Despair
_____ 4. Mysterious

5. The man ran up the stairs two at a time, shouting with ecstasy that he had won a million dollars.

_____ 1. Sympathy
_____ 2. Fear
_____ 3. Joy
_____ 4. Anger

(Continued)

6. The winners of the Super Bowl were shrieking, jumping up and down, and patting each other on the back.

  _x_ 1. Happiness
  ____ 2. Worry
  ____ 3. Despair
  ____ 4. Tense

7. Nyette walked along the beach enjoying the many colors of the sunset and the stillness of the hour.

  _x_ 1. Peace and quiet
  ____ 2. Worry
  ____ 3. Mysterious
  ____ 4. Solemn

8. The church bells tolled, the drums rolled, and men and women bowed their heads as the soldiers marched through the town.

  ____ 1. Fear
  ____ 2. Quiet
  ____ 3. Joy
  _x_ 4. Solemn

9. Greg's knuckles were white, his face ashen as he clung to the ledge, 100 stories over Sixth Avenue.

  _x_ 1. Fear
  ____ 2. Solemn
  ____ 3. Exciting
  ____ 4. None of the above

10. Andy's parents smiled and their eyes twinkled as they heard his name called at the graduation exercises.

  _x_ 1. Happiness
  ____ 2. Peace
  ____ 3. Mysterious
  ____ 4. None of the above

MASTERY REQUIREMENT: 8 correct responses

Indicate mastery on the student response sheet with a check.

6. The winners of the Super Bowl were shrieking, jumping up and down, and patting each other on the back.

____ 1. Happiness
____ 2. Worry
____ 3. Despair
____ 4. Tense

7. Nyette walked along the beach enjoying the many colors of the sunset and the stillness of the hour.

____ 1. Peace and quiet
____ 2. Worry
____ 3. Mysterious
____ 4. Solemn

8. The church bells tolled, the drums rolled, and men and women bowed their heads as the soldiers marched through the town.

____ 1. Fear
____ 2. Quiet
____ 3. Joy
____ 4. Solemn

9. Greg's knuckles were white, his face ashen as he clung to the ledge, 100 stories over Sixth Avenue.

____ 1. Fear
____ 2. Solemn
____ 3. Exciting
____ 4. None of the above

10. Andy's parents smiled and their eyes twinkled as they heard his name called at the graduation exercises.

____ 1. Happiness
____ 2. Peace
____ 3. Mysterious
____ 4. None of the above

FOURTH LEVEL

III. COMPREHENSION C. Creative Reading 4. Able to identify author's purpose

OBJECTIVE: The pupil will demonstrate the ability to identify the author's purpose.

DIRECTION: Read the selections and place an X in front of the phrase that indicates the author's purpose.

1. Zoey is a first-class dog food. Dogs who eat Zoey have shiny coats, bark with a deep tone, and never bite the postman. Go to the store today and buy Zoey for your dog.

   ____ a. To retell an incident
   _x_ b. To convince
   ____ c. To explain how to do something
   ____ d. To give information

2. Experts who study people and their work habits have made a recent statement about "schmoozing." Schmoozing is a German word. Schmoozing is what experts call the time that workers spend talking to their fellow workers, taking a long lunch, or making personal telephone calls during the work day.

   ____ a. To retell an incident
   ____ b. To convince
   ____ c. To explain how to do something
   _x_ d. To give information

3. Melt the chocolate in a pan of hot water. Pour the melted chocolate into a creamed mixture of eggs, sugar, and cream. When the mixture is blended, place in a plastic container. Freeze the chocolate cream and serve in two hours.

   ____ a. To retell an incident
   ____ b. To convince
   _x_ c. To explain how to do something
   ____ d. To give information

4. I hurried to get my work done so that I would have time to go swimming. I dashed to my room and changed from my jeans to my swimming suit. I ran down the stairs, out the door, and over to the pool. I was very excited for at last I would soon be in the pool. My towel was tossed onto a chair and the sky became cloudy. Within five minutes the sky was full of black clouds and that was the end of my swim.

   _x_ a. To retell an incident
   ____ b. To convince
   ____ c. To explain how to do something
   ____ d. To give information

5. Come to the Queen's Castle for the best steaks in the northwest. Whether you like your steak rare, medium or well done—we promise to please you. Atmosphere, good food, and a day you'll never forget are promised you at Queen's Castle.

   ____ a. To retell an incident
   _x_ b. To convince
   ____ c. To explain how to do something
   ____ d. To give information

MASTERY REQUIREMENT: 4 correct responses

Indicate mastery on the student response sheet with a check.

FOURTH LEVEL

III. COMPREHENSION Name ____________________

C. Creative Reading

Date ____________________

4. Able to identify author's purpose

Mastery __________

DIRECTIONS: Read the selections and place and X in front of the phrase that indicates the author's purpose.

1. Zoey is a first-class dog food. Dogs who eat Zoey have shiny coats, bark with a deep tone, and never bite the postman. Go to the store today and buy Zoey for your dog.

   _____ a. To retell an incident
   _____ b. To convince
   _____ c. To explain how to do something
   _____ d. To give information

2. Experts who study people and their work habits have made a recent statement about "schmoozing." Schmoozing is a German word. Schmoozing is what experts call the time that workers spend talking to their fellow workers, taking a long lunch, or making personal telephone calls during the work day.

   _____ a. To retell an incident
   _____ b. To convince
   _____ c. To explain how to do something
   _____ d. To give information

3. Melt the chocolate in a pan of hot water. Pour the melted chocolate into a creamed mixture of eggs, sugar, and cream. When the mixture is blended, place in a plastic container. Freeze the chocolate cream and serve in two hours.

   _____ a. To retell an incident
   _____ b. To convince
   _____ c. To explain how to do something
   _____ d. To give information

4. I hurried to get my work done so that I would have time to go swimming. I dashed to my room and changed from my jeans to my swimming suit. I ran down the stairs, out the door, and over to the pool. I was very excited for at last I would soon be in the pool. My towel was tossed onto a chair and the sky became cloudy. Within five minutes the sky was full of black clouds and that was the end of my swim.

   _____ a. To retell an incident
   _____ b. To convince
   _____ c. To explain how to do something
   _____ d. To give information

5. Come to the Queen's Castle for the best steaks in the northwest. Whether you like your steak rare, medium, or well done—we promise to please you. Atmosphere, good food, and a day you'll never forget are promised you at Queen's Castle.

   _____ a. To retell an incident
   _____ b. To convince
   _____ c. To explain how to do something
   _____ d. To give information

FOURTH LEVEL

III. COMPREHENSION C. Creative Reading 5. Able to identify character traits

OBJECTIVE: The pupil will demonstrate the ability to identify character traits.

DIRECTIONS: Read the selections carefully. Select and write on the line under the selection the character trait you think is described in the selection. Use only one character trait for each selection.

Thoughtful	Honest	Cheerful
Friendly	Brave	Shy

1. Eddie tiptoed out of the room and closed the bedroom door as quietly as he could. Eddie really wanted his dad to play ball with him, but when he saw his dad asleep with his glasses on and a book in his hands, he realized how tired his father must be. So he went down to the den and played with his dog.

   Thoughtful

2. Terry walked out of the store counting her change. She recounted her money a second and a third time. By this time, Terry was a block away from the drug store. She stopped, frowned, and thought. Suddenly, she turned and ran back to the drug store. She entered the store and said, "By mistake, you gave me change for ten dollars instead of for five dollars."

   Honest

3. Kathryn watched the folks across the street unload the big moving van. She dashed into the house and asked her mother if she could bake molasses cookies. She mixed the ingredients and baked the cookies. The aroma was delicious. Afterwards, she placed some cookies in a plate and brought them to the new neighbors.

   Friendly

4. The house was quickly filled with smoke. Louise slowly inched her way along the floor dragging her little sister with her. Louise kept saying, "Don't cry, we will soon be out of here. Hold my hand." Slowly, painfully, the girls crawled across the room to the door. The breath of fresh air was beautiful. Louise had saved her sister and herself.

   Brave

MASTERY REQUIREMENT: 3 correct responses

Indicate mastery on the student response sheet with a check.

FOURTH LEVEL

III. COMPREHENSION Name ____________________

C. Creative Reading

Date ____________________

5. Able to identify character traits

Mastery __________

DIRECTIONS: Read the selections carefully. Select and write on the line under the selection the character trait you think is described in the selection. Use only one character trait for each selection.

Thoughtful	Honest	Cheerful
Friendly	Brave	Shy

1. Eddie tiptoed out of the room and closed the bedroom door as quietly as he could. Eddie really wanted his dad to play ball with him, but when he saw his dad asleep with glasses on and a book in his hands, he realized how tired his dad must be. So he went down to the den and played with his dog.

____

2. Terry walked out of the store counting her change. She recounted her money a second and a third time. By this time, Terry was a block away from the drug store. She stopped, frowned, and thought. Suddenly, she turned and ran back to the drug store. She entered the store and said, "By mistake, you gave me change for ten dollars instead of for five dollars."

____

3. Kathryn watched the folks across the street unload the big moving van. She dashed into the house and asked her mother if she could bake molasses cookies. She mixed the ingredients and baked the cookies. The aroma was delicious. Afterwards, she placed some cookies in a plate and brought them to the new neighbors.

____

4. The house was quickly filled with smoke. Louise slowly inched her way along the floor dragging her little sister with her. Louise kept saying, "Don't cry, we will soon be out of here. Hold my hand," Slowly, painfully, the girls crawled across the room to the door. The breath of fresh air was beautiful. Louise had saved her sister and herself.

____

FOURTH LEVEL

III. COMPREHENSION D. Formal Outlining 1. Form a. Main ideas (I, II, III)

OBJECTIVE: The pupil will demonstrate the ability to outline the main ideas of a selection.

DIRECTIONS: Read the following selection very carefully and outline the main idea of each paragraph.

Fireworks

Nothing is quite as spectacular as celebrating a holiday with fireworks. Independence Day, better known as the Fourth of July, in many places is climaxed with a fireworks display. But what sparkles can also be dangerous.

According to the United States Consumer Product Safety Commission, injuries related to fireworks are increasing every year. Thousands of people are rushed to emergency hospital units for firework-related injuries. Most of the injuries occur to children under the age of fifteen. The injuries most likely to be reported are blindness, loss of limbs, and burns.

As a result of severe injuries increasing in number, the federal government has prohibited the sale of cherry bombs, aerial bombs, M-80 salutes, and firecrackers containing more than 2 millograms of powder. The fuses may burn at least three seconds but no longer than six seconds.

The first safety rule in using fireworks is read the directions. Do not take fireworks apart. Light only one firework at a time and never light them in metal or glass containers. Fireworks, even sparklers, should not be used by very small children. Fireworks should not be thrown from or into a vehicle.

Play it safe–do not use fireworks yourself. Attend fireworks displays sponsored by organizations in your town. These displays are generally conducted under the close supervision of men who know what they are doing.

Outline:

I: Fireworks are used to celebrate holidays
II: Many injuries result from fireworks every year
III: The federal government prohibits the sale of certain kinds of fireworks
IV: Follow safety rules in using fireworks
V: Do not use fireworks yourself, but watch other groups' displays

MASTERY REQUIREMENT: All correct, but the wording may be different from the above.

Indicate mastery on the student response sheet with a check.

FOURTH LEVEL

III. COMPREHENSION — Name ______________________

D. Formal Outlining

Date ______________________

1. Form

a. Main ideas (I, II, III) — Mastery __________

DIRECTIONS: Read the following selection very carefully and outline the main idea of each paragraph.

Fireworks

Nothing is quite as spectacular as celebrating a holiday with fireworks. Independence Day, better known as the Fourth of July, in many places is climaxed with a fireworks display. But what sparkles can also be dangerous.

According to the United States Consumer Product Safety Commission, injuries related to fireworks are increasing every year. Thousands of people are rushed to emergency hospital units for firework-related injuries. Most of the injuries occur to children under the age of fifteen. The injuries most likely to be reported are blindness, loss of limbs, and burns.

As a result of severe injuries increasing in number, the federal government has prohibited the sale of cherry bombs, aerial bombs, M-80 salutes, and firecrackers containing more than 2 millograms of powder. The fuses may burn at least three seconds but no longer than six seconds.

The first safety rule in using fireworks is read the directions. Do not take fireworks apart. Light only one firework at a time and never light them in metal or glass containers. Fireworks, even sparklers, should not be used by very small children. Fireworks should not be thrown from or into a vehicle.

Play it safe—do not use fireworks yourself. Attend fireworks displays sponsored by organizations in your town. These displays are generally conducted under the close supervision of men who know what they are doing.

Outline:

I: ______________________

II: ______________________

III: ______________________

IV. ______________________

V. ______________________

FOURTH LEVEL

III. COMPREHENSION D. Formal Outlining 1. Form b. Subordinate ideas (A, B, C)

OBJECTIVE: The pupil will demonstrate the ability to outline subordinate ideas.

DIRECTIONS: Read the following selection and fill in the outline.

Walking

Exercising is something everyone should do. Lately, more people, young and old, are exercising than ever before. Some jog, leaving them breathless. Some have regular exercise programs they perform. Others swim, golf, play tennis, or ride bicycles. The name of the game is keeping one's body in good condition.

The exercise that is available to nearly everyone and one that everybody can afford is walking. Walking does not require any expensive equipment, no special outfit and can be done wherever you are. Walking is an exercise available to rich and poor, tall and short, fat or thin, young and old. Walking is so available, it's easily overlooked. It's right at the bottom of your body.

What kind of equipment does one need for walking? A good pair of walking shoes is all you need. You can wear jeans, shorts, slacks, or whatever you wish. No uniform is needed. Shoes should be comfortable and have a low heel. A shoe with a spongy sole will put a spring in your walk.

There are tips to follow for those who plan to be walkers. As with any other exercise, don't overdo at the beginning. Start with short walks and build up slowly. Take a walk in different directions for a little variety. Walk briskly and with a purpose. Walking is good for your heart as well as for other muscles of your body.

Other effects of walking besides toning your muscles is that you can learn about the area where you walk. You may be surprised at the number of your friends you meet out walking. Walking is a good time for thinking and letting your mind wander. Walking can be fun if you make it so. As the ads say—Try it. You may like it.

I. Exercising is for everyone
    A. More people exercise every day
    B. Some swim, jog, golf, play tennis
    C. The goal is keep the body in good condition
II. Walking is an exercise available to all
    A. Not expensive
    B. Needs no special outfit
    C. Can be done everywhere
III. Equipment needed for walking
    A. Comfortable pair of shoes
    B. No special uniform
IV. Tips for walkers
    A. Don't overdo at the beginning
    B. Start with short walks
    C. Walk in different directions
    D. Walk briskly
V. Effects of walking
    A. Tones the muscles
    B. Learn about the area
    C. Meet friends

MASTERY REQUIREMENT: Teacher discretion or 16 correct responses

Indicate mastery on the student response sheet with a check.

FOURTH LEVEL

III. COMPREHENSION **Name**________________________

D. Formal Outlining

Date ________________________

1. Form

b. Subordinate ideas (A, B, C) **Mastery** __________

DIRECTIONS: Read the following selection and fill in the outline.

Walking

Exercising is something everyone should do. Lately, more people, young and old, are exercising than ever before. Some jog, leaving them breathless. Some have regular exercise programs they perform. Others swim, golf, play tennis, or ride bicycles. The name of the game is keeping one's body in good condition.

The exercise that is available to nearly everyone and one that everybody can afford is walking. Walking does not require any expensive equipment, no special outfit and can be done wherever you are. Walking is an exercise available to rich and poor, tall and short, fat or thin, young and old. Walking is so available, it's easily overlooked. It's right at the bottom of your body.

What kind of equipment does one need for walking? A good pair of walking shoes is all you need. You can wear jeans, shorts, slacks, or whatever you wish. No uniform is needed. Shoes should be comfortable and have a low heel. A shoe with a spongy sole will put a spring in your walk.

There are tips to follow for those who plan to be walkers. As with any other exercise, don't overdo at the beginning. Start with short walks and build up slowly. Take a walk in different directions for a little variety. Walk briskly and with a purpose. Walking is good for your heart as well as for other muscles of your body.

Other effects of walking besides toning your muscles is that you can learn about the area where you walk. You may be surprised at the number of your friends you meet out walking. Walking is a good time for thinking and letting your mind wander. Walking can be fun if you make it so. As the ads say—Try it. You may like it.

I. ________________________
   A. ________________________
   B. ________________________
   C. ________________________

II. ________________________
   A. ________________________
   B. ________________________
   C. ________________________

III. ________________________
   A. ________________________
   B. ________________________

IV. ________________________
   A. ________________________
   B. ________________________
   C. ________________________
   D. ________________________

V. ________________________
   A. ________________________
   B. ________________________
   C. ________________________

FOURTH LEVEL

III. COMPREHENSION D. Formal Outlining 2. Talking from an outline

OBJECTIVE: The pupil will demonstrate the ability to talk from an outline.

DIRECTIONS: Tell the student that the assignment is to outline a topic and then give a presentation. The topic can be assigned, or the student may be permitted to select his/her own. The topic may be a recent news item, a science subject, a general interest item, or a topic from a correlated unit of study. The student's presentation may be either to you or to the class.

MASTERY REQUIREMENT: Teacher discretion

Indicate mastery on the student response sheet with a check.

FOURTH LEVEL

III. COMPREHENSION

D. Formal Outlining

2. Talking from an outline

Name ______________________________

Date ______________________________

Mastery ____________

DIRECTIONS: After a topic has been selected, outline the topic and prepare an oral presentation to be given to ________________________ using your outline for the presentation.

____

____

____

____

____

____

____

____

____

____

FOURTH LEVEL

IV. ORAL AND SILENT READING   A. Understands Material at Grade Level

OBJECTIVE: The pupil will demonstrate an understanding of material read at grade level.

DIRECTIONS: Option I: Have the pupil read a selection from a basal reader or other subject area text. Ask a few questions to determine the pupil's comprehension.

Option II: Read the following selection and answer the questions by filling in the blanks.

The Mosquito

My mother has told me many times not to let little things bother me. But have you ever tried to sleep with one little mosquito buzzing around? The buzz, buzz keeps you awake. You swat where you think it is only to find that the little pest is somewhere else. Soon you start itching and you may not even be bitten.

I have never known anyone who enjoys a pest, and a mosquito is really a pest. But it is not just a pest. It can transmit diseases.

Mosquitoes deposit their eggs on the banks of creeks and reservoirs or other damp places—any place with still water. The egg stage lasts several days and is followed by a seven-day larvae stage. Larvae become pupae for the final two or three days before the insects are considered adults.

Only the female mosquito bites. The female bites because she needs a blood meal to provide the protein nutrient necessary for her eggs.

Strange as it may seem, moquitoes are more attracted to darker skinned people than they are to those with light skin. They are also attracted by movement. Insect repellents have been found to help keep mosquitoes away. So the next time you hear buzz, buzz, get a can of insect repellent and go psst, psst.

1. What is the little thing that bothers the writer?

   the mosquito

2. Where do mosquitoes deposit their eggs?

   in damp places

3. How long does the egg stage last?

   several days

4. Why does the female mosquito bite?

   to provide the protein nutrient needed for her eggs

5. What attracts mosquitoes?

   dark skin and movement

MASTERY REQUIREMENT: 4 correct responses

Indicate mastery on the student response sheet with a check.

FOURTH LEVEL

IV. ORAL AND SILENT READING

A. Understands Material at Grade Level

Name ______________________

Date ______________________

Mastery __________

DIRECTIONS: Read the following selection and answer the questions by filling in the blanks.

The Mosquito

My mother told me many times not to let little things bother me. But have you ever tried to sleep with one little mosquito buzzing around? The buzz, buzz keeps you awake. You swat where you think it is only to find that the little pest is somewhere else. Soon you start itching and you may not even be bitten.

I have never known anyone who enjoys a pest, and a mosquito is really a pest. But it is not just a pest. It can transmit diseases.

Mosquitoes deposit their eggs on the banks of creeks and reservoirs or other damp places—any place with still water. The egg stage lasts several days and is followed by a seven-day larvae stage. Larvae become pupae for the final two or three days before the insects are considered adults.

Only the female mosquito bites. The female bites because she needs a blood meal to provide the protein nutrient necessary for her eggs.

Strange as it may seem, mosquitoes are more attracted to darker skinned people than they are to those with light skin. They are also attracted by movement. Insect repellents have been found to help keep mosquitoes away. So the next time you hear buzz, buzz, buzz, get a can of insect repellent and go psst, psst.

1. What is the little thing that bothers the writer?

____

2. Where do mosquitoes deposit their eggs?

____

3. How long does the egg stage last?

____

4. Why does the female mosquito bite?

____

5. What attracts mosquitoes?

____

FOURTH LEVEL

IV. ORAL AND SILENT READING B. Eye-Voice Span of Three Words in Oral Reading

OBJECTIVE: The pupil will demonstrate an eye-voice span of three words in oral reading.

DIRECTIONS: Option I: Have the student read a selection and observe the student's eye-voice span. Record the mastery of the skill on the student response sheet.

Option II: Assign the student a paragraph to read aloud. Permit the student to read the selection silently before the oral reading. Observe the student's eye-voice span as the selection is read aloud.

1. Momma,

   I bet you're thinking you finally got your birthday gift! Well, it's not always that easy! In other words, welcome to the birthday gift hunt! Hope you enjoy it!

   You may want to get a "snack" before you start your hunt!

   Love,
   Your daughter

2. Dear Lady H.,

   Congratulations! You've made it to the first hunting trail. And what a sign this is! I bet you are glad that I'm "buttering you up" for this. While you're here, like every good hunter, you might like to "wash up" before you go out on the trail.

   See you later partner!

3. Well good buddie,

   This here water-n-hole has been knowed for its habit of putting on "airs" as in false pretenses! I see as to where you got fooled too! But you'll feel better after you get a good evening's sleep out yonder in the "bunk"! Don't let them thar bugs get ye!

   Yorn Padner

4. Hey,

   No false pretenses here, just the "bar" facts! I hope you enjoy it. Sorry it took so long for you to find it. Hope you enjoyed the hunting trip.

   I love you,
   Marguerite

P.S. To the reader—Can you guess what the birthday gift was?
A door bar for exercising.

MASTERY REQUIREMENT: Teacher discretion

Indicate mastery on the student response sheet with a check.

FOURTH LEVEL

IV. ORAL AND SILENT READING **Name** ____________________

B. Eye-Voice Span of Three Words in Oral Reading **Date**____________________

Mastery ____________

DIRECTIONS: Option I: Read silently the selection assigned to you by the teacher. In a few minutes you will be requested to read it aloud.

Option II: Read the following paragraphs to yourself. Later you will read aloud one or more of the paragraphs.

1. Momma,

I bet you're thinking you finally got your birthday gift! Well, it's not always that easy! In other words, welcome to the birthday gift hunt! Hope you enjoy it!

You may want to get a "snack" before you start your hunt!

Love,
Your daughter

2. Dear Lady H.,

Congratulations! You've made it to the first hunting trail. And what a sign this is! I bet you are glad that I'm "buttering you up" for this. While you're here, like every good hunter, you might like to "wash up" before you go out on the trail.

See you later partner!

3. Well good buddie,

This here water-n-hole has been knowed for its habit of putting on "airs" as in false pretenses! I see as to where you got fooled too! But you'll feel better after you get a good evening's sleep out yonder in the "bunk"! Don't let them thar bugs get ye!

Yorn Padner

4. Hey,

No false pretenses here, just the "bar" facts! I hope you enjoy it. Sorry it took so long for you to find it. Hope you enjoyed the hunting trip.

I love you,
Marguerite

P.S. To the reader–Can you guess what the birthday gift was? A door bar for exercising.

BARBE READING SKILLS CHECK LIST
FOURTH LEVEL

(Last Name) (First Name) (Name of School)

(Age) (Grade Placement) (Name of Teacher)

I. Vocabulary:

A. Word Recognition
1. Knows new words in content fields
2. Recognizes similarities of known words
   a. compound words
   b. root words
   c. suffixes, prefixes
   d. plurals
   e. hyphenated words
   f. contractions
3. Recognizes unusual characteristics of words

B. Word Meaning
1. Develops ability in getting meaning from context
2. Uses new words in sentences to show meaning
3. Knows punctuation
   a. italics
   b. quotation marks
   c. parenthesis
   d. exclamation marks
4. Use of map skills

C. Review Dolch Words

II. Word Attack Skills:

A. Structural analysis
1. Knows and applies rules for syllables
   a. Each syllable must contain a vowel and a single vowel can be a syllable
   b. Suffixes and prefixes are syllables with meanings of their own
   c. The root word is not divided
   d. If the first vowel is followed by two consonants, the first syllable usually ends with the first consonant (example: pen cil)
   e. If the first vowel is followed by a single consonant, the consonant usually begins the second syllable (example: a maze, am ple)
   f. If a word ends in le preceded by a consonant, that consonant begins the last syllable
   g. The letter x always goes with the preceding vowel to form a syllable (example: ex it)
   h. The letters ck go with the preceding vowel and end the syllable (example: chick en)
2. Knows accent clues
   a. The first syllable is usually accented, unless it is a prefix
   b. Beginning syllables de, re, be, in and a are usually unaccented
   c. Endings that form syllables are usually unaccented (run ning)
   d. ck following a single vowel is accented (example: jack et)
3. Knows suffixes and prefixes:
   a. Suffixes:

ness	(being)	sickness
ment	(result of)	movement
ward	(in direction of)	backward
ous	(full of)	joyous
ious	(abounding in)	gracious
et	(little)	leaflet
able	(capable of being)	capable
ic	(like, made of)	magic
ish	(like)	foolish
ant	(being)	vacant
ent	(one who)	president
age	(collection of)	baggage
ance	(state of being)	disturbance
ence	(state or quality)	violence
wise	(ways)	crosswise
ling	(little)	duckling
ty	(state)	unity
ure	(denoting action)	pleasure
ion	(condition or quality)	action

   b. Prefixes:

dis	(not, apart)	dismiss
in	(not)	invade
mis	(wrong)	mistake
anti	(against)	anticlimax
non	(not)	nonsense
com	(with)	combine
con	(with)	connect
pre	(before)	prepare
super	(over)	superior
tri	(three)	tricycle
sub	(under)	submarine
post	(after)	postscript
ab	(from)	abnormal
trans	(across)	translate
em	(in)	embark
de	(from)	depart
inter	(between)	interurban
pro	(in front of)	promote
ex	(out of or out)	explain
en	(in)	enter
ob	(against)	object
per	(fully, through)	perfect

B. Phonic analysis
1. Knows phonic skills
   a. Single consonants and blends
   b. Short and long vowels
   c. Vowel teams:

ee ___	au ___	oi ___
ea ___	aw ___	oy ___
ai ___	oa ___	ou ___
ay ___	oo ___	ow ___

2. Knows vowel rules
   a. In attacking a vowel sound try first the short sound; if the word then doesn't make sense try the long sound
   b. Vowels are usually short when they appear as single vowels and are followed by a consonant
   c. Vowels are usually given the long sound when they appear alone and are the last letters of a word
   d. When two vowels appear together in a word, the first vowel is long and the second is silent
   e. In short word containing two vowels where one of the vowels is a final e, the first vowel will have a long sound while the final e is silent

C. Uses dictionary and glossary
1. Alphabetical Order:
   a. Order of letters in alphabet
   b. Alphabetical arrangement of words
2. Knows to divide the dictionary to determine in which 1/3 or 1/4 the word may be found
3. Knows the meaning and use of the phonetic spelling that follows in parenthesis each word in the dictionary
4. Knows the use of the pronunciation key
5. Knows to select the meaning which fits best according to the context in which the word is used
6. Knows the meaning and use of guide words
7. Knows the meaning and use of the secondary accent mark

III. Comprehension:

A. Finding the main idea
1. Choosing title for material read
2. Can identify key words and topic sentences
3. Summarizing

B. Finding details
1. Finding specific information
2. Interpreting descriptive words and phrases
3. Selecting facts to remember
4. Selecting facts to support main idea
5. Using study guides, charts, outlines
6. Verifying answers
7. Arranging ideas in sequence

C. Creative reading
1. Able to interpret story ideas (generalize)
2. Able to see relationships
3. Able to identify the mood of a reading selection
4. Able to identify author's purpose
5. Able to identify character traits

D. Formal outlining
1. Form
   a. Main ideas (I, II, III)
   b. Subordinate ideas (A, B, C)
2. Talking from an outline

IV. Oral and Silent Reading:

A. Understands material at grade level

B. Eye-voice span of three words in oral reading

BARBE READING SKILLS CHECK LIST
FOURTH LEVEL

(Last Name) ______ (First Name) ______ (Name of School) ______

(Age) ______ (Grade Placement) ______ (Name of Teacher) ______

I. Vocabulary:

A. Word Recognition
1. Knows new words in content fields
2. Recognizes similarities of known words
   a. compound words
   b. root words
   c. suffixes, prefixes
   d. plurals
   e. hyphenated words
   f. contractions
3. Recognizes unusual characteristics of words

B. Word Meaning
1. Develops ability in getting meaning from context
2. Uses new words in sentences to show meaning
3. Knows punctuation
   a. italics
   b. quotation marks
   c. parenthesis
   d. exclamation marks
4. Use of map skills

C. Review Dolch Words

II. Word Attack Skills:

A. Structural analysis
1. Knows and applies rules for syllables
   a. Each syllable must contain a vowel and a single vowel can be a syllable
   b. Suffixes and prefixes are syllables with meanings of their own
   c. The root word is not divided
   d. If the first vowel is followed by two consonants, the first syllable usually ends with the first consonant (example: pen cil)
   e. If the first vowel is followed by a single consonant, the consonant usually begins the second syllable (example: a maze, am ple)
   f. If a word ends in le preceded by a consonant, that consonant begins the last syllable
   g. The letter x always goes with the preceding vowel to form a syllable (example: ex it)
   h. The letters ck go with the preceding vowel and end the syllable (example: chick en)
2. Knows accent clues
   a. The first syllable is usually accented, unless it is a prefix
   b. Beginning syllables de, re, be, in and a are usually unaccented
   c. Endings that form syllables are usually unaccented (run ning)
   d. ck following a single vowel is accented (example: jack et)
3. Knows suffixes and prefixes:
   a. Suffixes:

ness	(being)	sickness
ment	(result of)	movement
ward	(in direction of)	backward
ous	(full of)	joyous
ious	(abounding in)	gracious
et	(little)	leaflet
able	(capable of being)	capable
ic	(like, made of)	magic
ish	(like)	foolish
ant	(being)	vacant
ent	(one who)	president
age	(collection of)	baggage
ance	(state of being)	disturbance
ence	(state or quality)	violence
wise	(ways)	crosswise
ling	(little)	duckling
ty	(state)	unity
ure	(denoting action)	pleasure
ion	(condition or quality)	action

   b. Prefixes:

dis	(not, apart)	dismiss
in	(not)	invade
mis	(wrong)	mistake
anti	(against)	anticlimax
non	(not)	nonsense
com	(with)	combine
con	(with)	connect
pre	(before)	prepare
super	(over)	superior
tri	(three)	tricycle
sub	(under)	submarine
post	(after)	postscript
ab	(from)	abnormal
trans	(across)	translate
em	(in)	embark
de	(from)	depart
inter	(between)	interurban
pro	(in front of)	promote
ex	(out of or out)	explain
en	(in)	enter
ob	(against)	object
per	(fully, through)	perfect

B. Phonic analysis
1. Knows phonic skills
   a. Single consonants and blends
   b. Short and long vowels
   c. Vowel teams:

ee ___	au ___	oi ___
ea ___	aw ___	oy ___
ai ___	oa ___	ou ___
ay ___	oo ___	ow ___

2. Knows vowel rules
   a. In attacking a vowel sound try first the short sound; if the word then doesn't make sense try the long sound
   b. Vowels are usually short when they appear as single vowels and are followed by a consonant
   c. Vowels are usually given the long sound when they appear alone and are the last letters of a word
   d. When two vowels appear together in a word, the first vowel is long and the second is silent
   e. In short word containing two vowels where one of the vowels is a final e, the first vowel will have a long sound while the final e is silent

C. Uses dictionary and glossary
1. Alphabetical Order:
   a. Order of letters in alphabet
   b. Alphabetical arrangement of words
2. Knows to divide the dictionary to determine in which 1/3 or 1/4 the word may be found
3. Knows the meaning and use of the phonetic spelling that follows in parenthesis each word in the dictionary
4. Knows the use of the pronunciation key
5. Knows to select the meaning which fits best according to the context in which the word is used
6. Knows the meaning and use of guide words
7. Knows the meaning and use of the secondary accent mark

III. Comprehension:

A. Finding the main idea
1. Choosing title for material read
2. Can identify key words and topic sentences
3. Summarizing

B. Finding details
1. Finding specific information
2. Interpreting descriptive words and phrases
3. Selecting facts to remember
4. Selecting facts to support main idea
5. Using study guides, charts, outlines
6. Verifying answers
7. Arranging ideas in sequence

C. Creative reading
1. Able to interpret story ideas (generalize)
2. Able to see relationships
3. Able to identify the mood of a reading selection
4. Able to identify author's purpose
5. Able to identify character traits

D. Formal outlining
1. Form
   a. Main ideas (I, II, III)
   b. Subordinate ideas (A, B, C)
2. Talking from an outline

IV. Oral and Silent Reading:

A. Understands material at grade level

B. Eye-voice span of three words in oral reading

BARBE READING SKILLS CHECK LIST
FOURTH LEVEL

(Last Name) (First Name) (Name of School)

(Age) (Grade Placement) (Name of Teacher)

I. Vocabulary:
A. Word Recognition
1. Knows new words in content fields
2. Recognizes similarities of known words
a. compound words
b. root words
c. suffixes, prefixes
d. plurals
e. hyphenated words
f. contractions
3. Recognizes unusual characteristics of words
B. Word Meaning
1. Develops ability in getting meaning from context
2. Uses new words in sentences to show meaning
3. Knows punctuation
a. italics
b. quotation marks
c. parenthesis
d. exclamation marks
4. Use of map skills
C. Review Dolch Words

II. Word Attack Skills:
A. Structural analysis
1. Knows and applies rules for syllables
a. Each syllable must contain a vowel and a single vowel can be a syllable
b. Suffixes and prefixes are syllables with meanings of their own
c. The root word is not divided
d. If the first vowel is followed by two consonants, the first syllable usually ends with the first consonant [illegible]
e. [illegible]
f. [illegible]
g. The letter [illegible] vowel [illegible]
h. [illegible]
2. Knows accent [illegible]
a. The first syllable is usually accented, unless it [illegible]
b. [illegible]
c. Endings that form syllables are usually unaccented [illegible]
d. [illegible] a single vowel [illegible]
3. Knows suffixes and prefixes
a. Suffixes:

ness	(being)	sickness
ment	(result of)	movement
ward	(in direction of)	backward
ous	(full of)	joyous
ious	(abounding in)	gracious
et	(little)	leaflet
able	(capable of being)	capable
ic	(like, made of)	magic
ish	(like)	foolish
ant	(being)	vacant
ent	(one who)	president
age	(collection of)	baggage
ance	(state of being)	disturbance
ence	(state or quality)	violence
wise	(ways)	crosswise
ling	(little)	duckling
ty	(state)	unity
ure	(denoting action)	pleasure
ion	(condition or quality)	action

b. Prefixes:

dis	(not, apart)	dismiss
in	(in)	invade
mis	(wrong)	mistake
anti	(against)	anticlimax
non	(not)	nonsense
com	(with)	combine
con	(with)	connect
pre	(before)	prepare
super	(over)	superior
tri	(three)	tricycle
sub	(under)	submarine
post	(after)	postscript
ab	(from)	abnormal
trans	(across)	translate
em	(in)	embark
de	(from)	depart
inter	(between)	interurban
pro	(in front of)	promote
ex	(out of or out)	explain
en	(in)	enter
ob	(against)	object
per	(fully, through)	perfect

B. Phonic analysis
1. Knows phonic skills
a. Single consonants and blends
b. Short and long vowels
c. Vowel teams

ee ___	au ___	oi ___
ea ___	aw ___	ey ___
ai ___	oa ___	oo ___
ay ___	ou ___	ow ___

2. Knows vowel rules
a. In attacking a vowel sound try first the short sound, if the word then doesn't make sense try the long sound
b. Vowels are usually short when they appear as single vowels and are followed by a consonant
c. Vowels are usually given the long sound when they appear alone and are the last letters of a word
d. [illegible] two vowels appear together in a word, the [illegible] the long [illegible] and the second is silent
e. [illegible] containing two vowels [illegible] of which is final e, the first vowel will have a long sound while the final e is silent
C. Uses dictionary and glossary
1. Alphabetical order
a. Order of letters in alphabet
b. Alphabetical arrangement of words
2. Knows to divide the dictionary to determine in which 1/3 or 1/4 the word may be found.
3. Knows the meaning and use of the phonetic spelling that follows in parenthesis each word in the dictionary
4. Knows the use of the pronunciation key
5. [illegible] the meaning which is best according to the context in which the word is used
6. Knows the meaning and use of [illegible] words
7. Knows the meaning and use of the secondary accent mark

III. Comprehension:
A. Finding the main idea
1. Choosing title for material read
2. Can identify key words and topic sentences
3. Summarizing
B. Finding details
1. Finding specific information
2. Interpreting descriptive words and phrases
3. Selecting facts to remember
4. Selecting facts to support main idea
5. Using study guides, charts, outlines
6. Verifying answers
7. Arranging ideas in sequence
C. Creative reading
1. Able to interpret story ideas (generalize)
2. Able to see relationships
3. Able to identify the mood of a reading selection
4. Able to identify author's purpose
5. Able to identify character traits
D. Formal outlining
1. Form
a. Main ideas (I, II, III)
b. Subordinate ideas (A, B, C)
2. Taking notes from an outline

IV. Oral and Silent Reading:
A. Understands material at grade level
B. Eye-voice span of three words in oral reading